Biography Today

Profiles of People of Interest to Young Readers

World Leaders Series: Environmental Leaders

Vol. 1
1997

Kevin Hillstrom
Laurie Hillstrom,
Editors

Omnigraphics, Inc.

Penobscot Building
Detroit, MI 48226

Kevin Hillstrom and Laurie Hillstrom, *Editors*

Biography Today Series
Laurie Lanzen Harris, *Executive Editor*
Cherie D. Abbey, *Associate Editor*
Barry Puckett, Research *Associate*

Omnigraphics, Inc.

* * *

Matt Barbour, *Production Manager*
Laurie Lanzen Harris, *Vice President, Editorial Director*
Peter E. Ruffner, *Vice President, Administration*
James A. Sellgren, *Vice President, Operations and Finance*
Jane Steele, *Marketing Consultant*

* * *

Frederick G. Ruffner, Jr., Publisher

Contents

Preface

By dedicating their lives to preserving and protecting the environment, each of the men and women profiled in *Biography Today: Environmental Leaders* has had a lasting effect on the type of world that today's students will inherit. For example, young people will be able to explore expanses of pristine wilderness in the American West because of David Brower, and they will be able to hear wolves howling in Yellowstone National Park thanks to Renee Askins. The environmental leaders covered in this book come from a variety of backgrounds — including scientists, writers, political activists, and ordinary citizens — and have applied different tactics and methodologies to their conservation efforts. Their stories will provide students with information on a wide range of conservation issues and, we hope, inspire them to find their own ways of contributing to the environmental movement. "I know a lot of young people will appreciate this country, if given a chance. But they can't if the country isn't there. It all comes back to what things we think are important in life," said Margaret Murie, whose efforts helped establish Arctic National Wildlife Refuge in Alaska. "Every citizen has a responsibility toward this planet. I'm counting on the new generation coming up. I have to believe in their spirit as those who came before me believed in mine."

Kevin Hillstrom
Laurie Hillstrom
January 1997

Preface

Welcome to the first volume of the new **Biography Today World Leaders Series: Environmental Leaders**. We are publishing this new series in response to the growing number of suggestions from our readers, who want more coverage of more people in *Biography Today*. Six new volumes, covering **Authors, Artists, Environmental Leaders, Scientists and Inventors, Sports Figures, and World Leaders,** will be appearing in 1997. Each of these hardcover volumes will be 200 pages in length and cover approximately 15 individuals of interest to readers aged 9 and above. The length and format of the entries will be like those found in the regular issues of *Biography Today*, but there will be **no** duplication between the regular series and the special subject volumes.

The Plan of the Work

As with the regular issues of *Biography Today*, this special subject volume on **Environmental Leaders** was especially created to appeal to young readers in a format they can enjoy reading and readily understand. Each volume contains alphabetically arranged sketches. Each entry provides at least one picture of the individual profiled, and bold-faced rubrics lead the reader to information on birth, youth, early memories, education, first jobs, marriage and family, career highlights, memorable experiences, hobbies, and honors and awards. Each of the entries ends with a list of easily accessible sources designed to lead the student to further reading on the individual and a current address. Obituary entries are also included, written to provide a perspective on the individual's entire career. Obituaries are clearly marked in both the table of contents and at the beginning of the entry.

Biographies are prepared by Omnigraphics editors after extensive research, utilizing the most current materials available. Those sources that are generally available to students appear in the list of further reading at the end of the sketch.

Indexes

To provide easy access to entries, each issue of the regular *Biography Today* series and each volume of the Special Subject Series contains a Name Index, General Index covering occupations, organizations, and ethnic and minority origins, Places of Birth Index, and a Birthday Index. These indexes cumulate with each succeeding volume or issue. Each of the Special Subject Volumes will be indexed as part of these cumulative indexes, so that readers can locate information on all individuals covered in either the regular or the special volumes.

Our Advisors

Biography Today was reviewed by an Advisory Board comprised of librarians, children's literature specialists, and reading instructors so that we could make sure that the concept of this publication—to provide a readable and accessible biographical magazine for young readers—was on target. They evaluated the title as it developed, and their suggestions have proved invaluable. Any errors, however, are ours alone. We'd like to list the Advisory Board members, and to thank them for their efforts.

Lee Sprince	Broward West Regional Library
	Fort Lauderdale, FL
Susan Stewart	Birney Middle School Reading Laboratory, Retired
	Southfield, MI
Ethel Stoloff	Librarian, Birney Middle School, Retired
	Southfield, MI

Our Advisory Board stressed to us that we should not shy away from controversial or unconventional people in our profiles, and we have tried to follow their advice. The Advisory Board also mentioned that the sketches might be useful in reluctant reader and adult literacy programs, and we would value any comments librarians might have about the suitability of our magazine for those purposes.

Your Comments Are Welcome

Our goal is to be accurate and up-to-date, to give young readers information they can learn from and enjoy. Now we want to know what you think. Take a look at this issue of *Biography Today*, on approval. Write or call me with your comments. We want to provide an excellent source of biographical information for young people. Let us know how you think we're doing.

And here's a special incentive: review our list of people to appear in upcoming issues. Use the bind-in card to list other people you want to see in *Biography Today*. If we include someone you suggest, your library wins a free issue, with our thanks. Please see the bind-in card for details.

Laurie Harris
Executive Editor, *Biography Today*

Edward Abbey   1927-1989
American Writer Whose Works Sparked
the Modern Environmental Movement
Author of *Desert Solitaire* and *The Monkey
Wrench Gang*

BIRTH

Edward Paul Abbey was born on January 29, 1927, in Indiana,
Pennsylvania. He was the oldest of five children born to Paul
Revere Abbey, a farmer, and Mildred Postlewaite Abbey, a
teacher. He had one sister, Nancy, and three brothers, one of
whom was named Howard.

YOUTH

Abbey spent his childhood in the small Appalachian farming community of Home, Pennsylvania. "We lived on this old farm that Ed called 'Old Lonesome Briar Patch,'" his sister Nancy recalled. "The birds, the animals, everything around us was something that my parents really loved and brought to us." As a boy, Abbey enjoyed hunting and fishing in the woods near his home. He also liked to write and draw, and he often created cartoon adventure stories to entertain his family.

Abbey turned 17 in 1944, when World War II was still going on. Certain that he would be drafted into the army the following year, after graduating from high school he decided to leave home for a few months and travel around the United States. "I was 17: wise, brown, ugly, shy, poetical; a bold, stupid, sun-dazzled kid, out to see the country before giving his life in the war against Japan," he noted. Before Abbey left on his trip, his father gave him $25 and told him, "Don't let anybody take you for a punk."

Abbey hitchhiked west, stopping every so often to work at odd jobs until he made enough money to continue his journey. He saw Yellowstone National Park in Wyoming, stopped briefly in Seattle, then went down the Pacific Coast to Yosemite National Park in northern California. But the highlight of his trip came when he hopped a ride on a freight train through Arizona and New Mexico. He was totally captivated by the stark desert landscape: "Crags and pinnacles of naked rock, the dark cores of ancient volcanoes, a vast and silent emptiness smoldering with heat, color, and indecipherable significance, above which floated a small number of pure, clear, hard-edged clouds," he recalled. "For the first time I felt I was getting close to the West of my deepest imaginings—the place where the tangible and the mythical become the same."

After three months on the road, Abbey finally became homesick. "I thought of the winding red-dog road that led under oak and maple trees toward the creaking farmhouse that was our home, where the dogs waited on the front porch, where my sister and my brothers played in the twilight under the giant sugar maple, where my father and mother sat inside in the amber light of kerosene lamps, listening to their battery-powered Zenith radio, waiting for me," he explained. In Albuquerque, New Mexico, he used the last of his money to buy a bus ticket back to Pennsylvania. True to his prediction, Abbey was drafted into the army shortly after his 18th birthday. He served as a military policeman in Italy for a year and received an honorable discharge in 1946.

EDUCATION

Thanks to the G.I. Bill (a government program that provided returning soldiers with money to attend college), Abbey began taking classes at Indiana

University of Pennsylvania in 1947. He still felt drawn to the West, however, so he transferred to the University of New Mexico (UNM) in 1948. It was during his college years that Abbey's radical political views first came to light. During a short stint as editor of the UNM literary magazine, *The Thunderbird,* he wrote an editorial in which he encouraged all the students to burn their draft cards in protest against the war in Korea. He also published an inflammatory quote on the cover of the magazine: "Man will never be free until the last king is strangled with the entrails of the last priest." Instead of attributing the quote to Voltaire, the French philosopher who actually said it, Abbey intentionally misattributed it to Louisa May Alcott, the American author of *Little Women* and other children's classics. As a result, Abbey was fired as editor of *The Thunderbird* and all copies of the magazine were seized and destroyed by the dean.

Despite his tendency to make trouble, Abbey earned his bachelor's degree in philosophy from UNM in 1951. He then received a Fulbright Fellowship to attend the University of Edinburgh in Scotland for a year. When he returned to the United States, he began a master's degree program at Yale University. He soon realized that his personality was not well-suited to the more conservative atmosphere of an Ivy League school, however, and ended up dropping out of Yale within two weeks. Abbey then returned to UNM, where his interest in radical political ideas continued to grow. By the time he earned his master's degree in philosophy in 1956, he considered himself an anarchist (a person who wants complete freedom and rebels against any kind of authority). In fact, his master's thesis was called "Anarchism and the Morality of Violence." Many years later, Abbey learned that his activities during college had earned him a place on the FBI's list of people to watch.

CAREER HIGHLIGHTS

After completing graduate school, Abbey spent the next 15 years doing seasonal work as a fire lookout or park ranger in several national parks and monuments, including Casa Grande and Sunset Crater in Arizona, Arches in Utah, and Glacier in Montana. Though he enjoyed the work, he was fired from many of his jobs because he tended to neglect his duties for days at a time in order to wander in the wilderness. Abbey also launched his writing career during these years. His first book, which he described as "a terrible novel called *Jonathan Troy,*" was published in 1956. It "made me think of myself as a writer," he noted, though "I really was not at that time. Didn't have the craft or the patience to write well."

His next few books were rejected by publishers. "I almost gave up at that point," Abbey admitted. "I gave serious thought to being a permanent, half-time park ranger." But then he got a break when the rights to his 1958 novel, *The Brave Cowboy*, were purchased by a Hollywood production company for $7,500. The book—about an anarchist cowboy who cuts fences in order to restore the West to open range—was turned into a film called *Lonely Are the Brave*, starring Kirk Douglas.

In 1959, Abbey had an experience that would change the focus of his writing for the rest of his life. He and a friend took a 10-day raft trip through Glen Canyon—a stunning, 2,000-foot gorge carved by the Colorado River in southern Utah—shortly before construction of the Glen Canyon Dam. Once the dam became operational, water backed up and flooded the entire canyon, turning it into what is now known as Lake Powell. "I was one of the lucky few (there could have been thousands more) who saw Glen Canyon before it was drowned," Abbey wrote. "In fact I saw only a part of it but enough to realize that here was an Eden, a portion of the earth's original paradise. To grasp the nature of the crime that was committed imagine the Taj Mahal or Chartres Cathedral buried in mud until only the spires remain visible. With this difference: those man-made celebrations of human aspiration could conceivably be reconstructed while Glen Canyon was a living thing, irreplaceable, which can never be recovered through any human agency." For Abbey, the huge concrete dam came to symbolize the destruction of the American West at the hands of greedy developers and government agencies. From that point on, he used his writing as part of a lifelong crusade to save the land he loved.

DESERT SOLITAIRE

One of Abbey's best-known and most influential books is *Desert Solitaire*, published in 1968. Most of the essays in the book were written during the two seasons Abbey spent as a park ranger at Arches National Monument (now Arches National Park) in the high desert of Utah. A combination of poetic description and angry criticism, Abbey's book shows both his deep love for nature and his bitter anger toward the various government and business interests that threatened to destroy it. Though it was not a great critical success at the time of its publication, *Desert Solitaire* has come to be considered a "classic ode to the disappearing West." One reviewer said that it "stands among the towering works of American nature writing."

In the book, Abbey saves some of his harshest criticism for tourists who drive through national parks in motor homes. "Industrial tourism is a threat to the national parks," he wrote. "But the chief victims of the system are the motorized tourists. They are being robbed and robbing themselves. So long as they are unwilling to crawl out of their cars they will not discover the treasures of the national parks and will never escape the stress and turmoil of those urban-suburban complexes which they had hoped, presumably, to leave behind for a while. How to pry the tourists out of their automobiles, out of their back-breaking upholstered mechanized wheelchairs and onto their feet, onto the strange warmth and solidity of Mother Earth again? This is the problem which the Park Service should confront."

To provide a better visitor experience and help restore the parks' natural beauty and serenity, Abbey recommended outlawing cars in the national parks. Instead, he suggested that people should leave their cars in lots outside the park boundaries and proceed on foot, by bicycle, on horseback, or in buses. "The motorized tourists, reluctant to give up the old ways, will complain that they can't see enough without their automobiles to bear them swiftly (traffic permitting) through the parks," he admitted. "But this is nonsense. A man on foot, on horseback or a bicycle will see more, feel more, enjoy more in a mile than the motorized tourists can in a hundred miles. Better to idle through one park in two weeks than try to race through a dozen in the same amount of time."

Desert Solitaire gained an immediate following among the large numbers of young people who were becoming concerned about the environment in the 1960s. Dave Foreman (see entry in this volume of *Biography Today*), founder of the radical environmental group Earth First!, explained how the book brought environmentalists together: "I can encounter people that I don't know when I give speeches and if they love the book *Desert Solitaire* like I do we're instantly friends and have an instant bond. There is a family of us out there, there is a clan of us out there. And I think the writings of Ed Abbey are the common denominator. They define a group of people in the West and we know we belong together. And that may have been Ed's real genius."

The success of *Desert Solitaire* took Abbey by surprise. He was suddenly in great demand to write articles and travel pieces for outdoor magazines. "I never wanted to be an environmental crusader, an environmental journalist. I wanted to be a fiction writer, a novelist," he explained. "Then I dashed off that *Desert Solitaire* thing because it was easy to do. All I did was copy out of some journals that I'd kept. It was the first book that I published that had any popularity at all, and at once I was put into the 'Western Environmentalist Writer' bag, category, pigeon hole. I haven't tried very hard to get out of it. I've been making a pretty easy living at it since then."

THE MONKEY WRENCH GANG

Abbey's influence grew with the publication of his novel *The Monkey Wrench Gang* in 1975. The book follows the adventures of four "environmental warriors"—an aging surgeon named Doc Sarvis, a hippie from New York named Bonnie Abbzug, a quiet Mormon mechanic known as Seldom Seen Smith, and a crude Vietnam veteran named George Washington Hayduke—who resort to desperate measures in their quest to save the West. Faced with the widespread destruction of land by mining, logging, and road-building operations, the gang goes on a comic crusade to sabotage these enterprises. They booby-trap trees with metal spikes that wreck chainsaws; they pour sand into the gas tanks of bulldozers so the engines will not start; and they tear down billboards and bridges. The ultimate target of the Monkey Wrench Gang is Glen Canyon Dam — Abbey's hated symbol of the ruin of the West — and they concoct an elaborate scheme to blow it up.

Though Abbey admitted that the characters in *The Monkey Wrench Gang* were based on some of his friends, he claimed that he borrowed certain aspects of their backgrounds or personalities and invented the rest. "Originally they were inspired by people I know, you might say that. But as I began writing the story they became more and more fictional, more and more imaginary," he stated. Abbey also admitted that he had taken part in some of the illegal exploits described in the book. "There was some field research involved in the creation of that book, yes," he noted. "You think the statute of limitations has run out?"

The Monkey Wrench Gang brought a new sense of urgency to the growing environmental movement. Many people suddenly recognized the extent of the threats facing the West and became committed to using any means necessary to protect it from further degradation. "As the wilderness crisis became much more severe, as the Forest Service began to destroy more areas, roads penetrated deeper into the wilderness, more clear cuts sprang up, a lot of folks realized that it was time to really implement the Monkey Wrench Gang," Foreman stated. This marked the beginning of "radical" environmental activism in the United States, as such groups as Earth First! and Greenpeace began using many of the tactics Abbey described to disrupt activities they viewed as harmful to the environment. The term "monkeywrenching" was applied to the acts of sabotage and vandalism that the activists employed to make their point.

With the publication of *The Monkey Wrench Gang,* Abbey became a role model and inspiration for many young activists. He also became the target of criticism for encouraging violence and destruction of property. Responding to such criticism, Abbey stated: "I believe that farming, ranching, mining, logging are all legitimate, honorable, useful and necessary enterprises. I respect and admire those who carry on these occupations. Especially those who do it in a way that treats the earth with love, and the rights of our posterity with respect. The problem, where things go wrong, is in scale, size, number. The carnage that we're doing to the American West, the planet as a whole, results, I think, mainly from too many people demanding more from the land than the land can sustain." He stood by the message of his book, proclaiming that "I regard defending the wilderness as something like defending your own home. I regard the wilderness

Edward Abbey with son Benjamin.

as my home, my true ancestral home. And when it's being invaded by clear cutters and strip miners, I feel not only the right but the duty, the moral obligation to defend it by any means I can."

Abbey argued that people need wilderness in order to feel happy, complete, and free—especially as society became more urbanized and automated. "We need wilderness because we are wild animals. Every man needs a place where he can go to go crazy in peace. Every Boy Scout troop deserves a forest to get lost, miserable, and starving in," he noted. "I take a dim view of dams; I find it hard to learn to love cement; I am poorly impressed by concrete aggregates and statistics in the cubic tons. But in this weakness I am not alone, for I belong to that ever-growing number of Americans, probably a good majority now, who have become aware that a fully industrialized, thoroughly urbanized, elegantly computerized social system is not suitable for human habitation. Great for machines, yes. But unfit for people."

"A man could be a lover and defender of the wilderness without ever in his lifetime leaving the boundaries of asphalt, powerlines, and right-angled surfaces. We need wilderness whether or not we ever set foot in it.

We need a refuge even though we may never need to go there. I may never in my life get to Alaska, for example, but I am grateful that it's there. We need the possibility of escape as surely as we need hope; without it the life of the cities would drive all men into crime or drugs or psychoanalysis," Abbey continued. "What makes life in our cities at once still tolerable, exciting, and stimulating is the existence of an alternative option, whether exercised or not, whether even appreciated or not, of a radically different mode of being *out there*, in the forests, on the lakes and rivers, in the deserts, up in the mountains."

DEATH AND LEGACY

In the early 1980s, Abbey began to feel ill. When he finally saw a doctor in 1982, he was diagnosed with pancreatic cancer. "Well, I guess I won't have to floss anymore," he told a friend after hearing the diagnosis. Fortunately, the diagnosis turned out to be wrong, but Abbey still suffered from a circulatory disorder that occasionally caused severe internal bleeding. He continued writing and traveling over the next few years, although he gradually became weaker and weaker. He died on March 14, 1989, at his home in Oracle, Arizona.

Since he knew that he was dying for some time, Abbey was able to leave detailed funeral instructions for his wife, Clarke Cartwright. He insisted that his body not be embalmed or placed in a coffin, but simply carried into the desert in the back of a pick-up truck and buried in an old sleeping bag. "I want my body to help fertilize the growth of a cactus or cliff rose or sagebrush or tree," he wrote. He also requested that his friends and family celebrate his life by throwing a raucous party, complete with a bonfire, beer, and corn on the cob. "No formal mourning, please—lots of singing, dancing, talking, hollering, laughing, and love-making instead," he stated. Abbey was buried in a private ceremony attended by about 200 close friends in Saguaro National Monument in Arizona. The location of his grave in the desert was never made public. It is marked only by a small stone tablet that reads, "Edward Paul Abbey, 1927-1989, No Comment."

During his lifetime, Abbey was called everything from "America's crankiest citizen" to "the godfather of modern environmental activism." He did not like to refer to himself as an environmentalist—"If a label is required, say that I am one who loves the unfenced country," he once wrote. Nevertheless, Abbey's passionate defense of wilderness in his more than 20 books inspired thousands of people to take up the cause. "A certain independent breed of reader preferred the passion, entertaining honesty, and unequaled passages of nature writing in an Abbey novel to the technically superior work of other writers," Susan Zakin wrote in *Coyotes and Town Dogs*. "He may not have reached the level of maturity attained by many great novelists, but by bringing his resonant and moving ideas about the primacy of nature into American discourse, the rebellious and erudite Abbey did more to change society than his contemporaries who produced better-honed work."

MARRIAGE AND FAMILY

Abbey was married five times and had five children. His first marriage, to Jean Schmechel while he was a undergraduate at the University of New Mexico, ended in divorce. He married Rita Deanim in 1952, and they had two sons together, Joshua and Aaron, before divorcing in 1965. Abbey married Judith Pepper later that year, and they had a daughter, Susannah, before Pepper died of leukemia in 1970. Abbey's next marriage, to Renee Downing, also ended in divorce. His fifth and final marriage, to Clarke Cartwright in 1982, produced two children, Rebecca and Benjamin.

WRITINGS

FICTION

Jonathan Troy, 1956
The Brave Cowboy, 1958
Fire on the Mountain, 1962
Black Sun, 1971
The Monkey Wrench Gang, 1975
Good News, 1980
The Fool's Progress, 1988
Hayduke Lives! 1990

NONFICTION

Desert Solitaire: A Season in the Wilderness, 1968
Appalachian Wilderness: The Great Smoky Mountains, 1970
Slickrock: The Canyon Country of Southeast Utah, 1971 (with Philip Hyde)
Cactus Country, 1973 (with others)
The Journey Home: Some Words in Defense of the American West, 1977
Back Roads of Arizona, 1978
The Hidden Canyon: A River Journey, 1978
Desert Images: An American Landscape, 1979 (with David Muench)
Abbey's Road: Take the Other, 1979
Down the River, 1982
In Praise of Mountain Lions, 1984 (with John Nichols)
Beyond the Wall: Essays from the Outside, 1984
Slumgullion Stew: An Edward Abbey Reader, 1984 (published as *The Best of Edward Abbey,* 1988)
One Life at a Time, Please, 1988
A Voice Crying in the Wilderness: Essays from a Secret Journal, 1990

HONORS AND AWARDS

Fulbright Fellowship: 1951
Western Heritage Award for Best Novel: 1963, for *Fire on the Mountain*
Guggenheim Fellowship: 1975
American Academy of Arts and Letters Award: 1987

FURTHER READING

BOOKS

Abbey, Edward. *Desert Solitaire: A Season in the Wilderness,* 1968
Benet's Reader's Encyclopedia of American Literature, 1991
Bishop, James. *Epitaph for a Desert Anarchist: The Life and Legacy of Edward Abbey,* 1994
Contemporary Authors, New Revision Series, Vol. 41
Contemporary Literary Criticism, Vol. 36
Hepworth, James, and Gregory McNamee, eds. *Resist Much, Obey Little: Some Notes on Edward Abbey,* 1985
Macrae, John, ed. *The Serpents of Paradise: A Reader,* 1995
McCann, Garth. *Edward Abbey,* 1977
Ronald, Ann. *The New West of Edward Abbey,* 1982
Wulbert, Roland, ed. *Confessions of a Barbarian: Selections from the Journals of Edward Abbey, 1951-1989,* 1994
Zakin, Susan. *Coyotes and Town Dogs: Earth First! and the Environmental Movement,* 1993

PERIODICALS

Backpacker, Oct. 1989, p.12; Sep. 1993, p.40
Los Angeles Times, Mar. 16, 1989, p.3
Mother Earth News, May-June 1984, p.17
New York Times, Mar. 15, 1989, p.D19
New York Times Book Review, May 7, 1989, p.44; Dec. 11, 1994, p.11
People Weekly, June 25, 1984, p.58
Utne Reader, July-Aug. 1989, p.36
Whole Earth Review, Winter 1988, p.17; Summer 1989, p.114

VIDEOTAPE

Edward Abbey: A Voice in the Wilderness, 1993

WORLD WIDE WEB SITE

http://www.utsidan.se/abbey/abbey.html

Renee Askins 1959-
American Scientist and Conservationist
Founder of the Wolf Fund
Led Effort to Reintroduce Wolves into
Yellowstone National Park

BIRTH

Renee Askins was born on January 19, 1959, near Boyne City, Michigan. Her parents were Raymond Askins, a businessman, and Chris Askins, a medical technician.

YOUTH AND EDUCATION

Askins developed her love for animals at an early age. She

spent many childhood hours roaming by herself through the woods of the Boyne City area, catching frogs and watching the other animals that made their home there. She loved to ride horses, too, and as she grew older she decided that she wanted a career that would allow her to continue to work with animals.

In 1977, after graduating from Boyne City High School, Askins enrolled at Kalamazoo College in southwestern Michigan. Over the next few years she worked very hard, and her life became a blur of studying and work, for she needed money to pay for her education. During one particularly exhausting summer spent in Washington State, she worked in a salmon cannery from 5:00 A.M. to 4:00 P.M. before going to a waitressing job at night. Despite her busy schedule, though, Askins kept her eye on her ultimate goal: securing a career in which she could study and help animals.

Askins was interested in all kinds of wildlife, but even as a college freshman, it was clear that wolves particularly fascinated her. Faced with finding a topic for a paper for one of her religion classes, she decided to write about the role of the wolf in different religious traditions and how the animal had come to be associated with the devil in some faiths.

In 1978 Askins continued her studies at a wolf research facility in Indiana. Before long she was spending almost all of her time watching captive wolves raise boisterous litters of pups. Askins was eventually given responsibility for one of the littlest pups, because its mother was having trouble taking care of it. Askins named the pup Natasha, and as she cared for the little wolf over the next few months, she marveled at its intelligence. "I kept a journal about her, but the whole time I felt like she was keeping her own journal about me," Askins recalled. "She had such dignity, and there was a level of sophistication and communication between her and the other wolves that I had never been aware of." Askins eventually returned to Kalamazoo to continue with her course work. She graduated from Kalamazoo College in 1981.

CAREER HIGHLIGHTS

Even though Askins had returned to Kalamazoo to continue with her course work, her experiences with Natasha and the other wolves at the Indiana facility had a lasting impact on her. Shortly after graduating, she promptly accepted a job offer from John Weaver, a Wyoming-based biologist who studied endangered species such as the wolf. As one of Weaver's assistants, Askins embraced the opportunity to work with and on behalf of wolves, bald eagles, mule deer, whooping cranes, great gray owls, and other endangered species. Her salary was terribly low — for about a year she lived in a tepee with her dog because she could not afford an apartment — but she found the work with Weaver to be both rewarding and educational.

In 1985 Askins arranged for a traveling exhibit called "Wolves and Humans: Competition, Coexistence, and Conflict" to be brought to Yellowstone National Park, where Weaver and his assistants did a lot of their research. The exhibit, which explained how the wolf population had been nearly destroyed by humans over the past 200 years, was a big success. It attracted more than 200,000 visitors, renewed calls for protection of wolves, and triggered a fundamental change in Askins's life. "It was a turning point for me," she said. "I saw I could do something concrete."

WAR ON THE WOLVES

Over the course of the last two centuries, North American wolves were driven to the verge of extinction by government officials and ranchers who were determined to wipe them out by any means necessary. Writer and park ranger Rick McIntyre pointed out in *A Society of Wolves* that "no one knows the number of wolves destroyed during our war on the species [but] naturalist Ernest Thompson Seton calculated that the wolf population of the lower 48 states was originally two million. By the 1950s, except for isolated populations of a few hundred wolves in the Upper Midwest, the gray wolf had been exterminated in the 48 states. From two million to a few hundred: The war against the wolf was one of the most successful programs ever carried out by the federal government."

The war was carried out not only because the wolf has long been viewed by ranchers and other businessmen as a threat to livestock and property, but also, according to Askins, because the wolf was seen as a powerful symbol of the untamed American wilderness. "We didn't just remove wolves that killed livestock," she noted. "The wars against predators at the turn of the century weren't about ridding ourselves of a nuisance; they were about the principle of dominance, and the wolf, the symbol of wild, untamable nature, was the object of conquest. We didn't just want to control wolves, we wanted to conquer them. So we didn't just kill wolves, we tortured them. We lassoed them and tore them apart by their limbs; we wired their jaws shut and left them to starve; we doused them with gasoline and ignited them."

RETURNING WOLVES TO YELLOWSTONE

Since the early 1980s, Askins had been helping Weaver with a campaign to reintroduce wolves into Yellowstone National Park. But when she saw the tremendous response to the "Wolves and Humans" exhibit, she decided to direct even more of her energy in that direction. "What I began to visualize and wanted to create was not an organization but a vehicle to accomplish a goal," she said. "I wanted to bring to conservation the sort of fresh ideas and imagination and passion I saw in art and in writing. With the level of rage and fear that surrounds this issue, you can't go into it in traditional ways." She thus launched the Wolf Fund, a group dedicated to one goal: the return of gray wolves into Yellowstone. "The day wolves return [to Yellowstone], the Wolf Fund will close its doors," Askins said.

Some people who knew of Askins's plans thought that the work of the Wolf Fund would have to be delayed for a few years, however, because Askins had already been accepted at the Yale School of Forestry and Environmental Studies. But even though her schooling took her thousands of miles away from Yellowstone, she worked hard on the Wolf Fund project. She appeared on behalf of the Wolf Fund at area universities and on the NBC Nightly News while simultaneously serving as its administrator and gathering the support of key environmentalists.

In 1988, after graduating with a master's degree in wildlife ecology, Askins rushed back to Wyoming to devote all her energy to returning wolves to Yellowstone. Her task was made easier by changes in public and government attitudes toward the animal that have taken place over the last few decades. In 1973 the wolf was designated an endangered species, and in 1987 the U.S. Fish and Wildlife Service initiated studies to determine whether or not wolves should be reintroduced into such places as Yellowstone. In addition, the wolf was increasingly recognized as an important factor in keeping such animals as moose and elk in balance with available food and habitat. Perhaps most importantly, though, public perceptions of wolves began to change. Previously seen as bloodthirsty predators, wolves were increasingly viewed as majestic symbols of the wild. Posters, sweatshirts, and books depicting them became bestselling items across the country.

Still, Askins knew that many people around Yellowstone and in other areas of the American West were very angry at the thought of returning wolves to wilderness lands that they had roamed in the past. She recognized that wolves had come to symbolize the ongoing battle in the American West between those who believe that the land is there to be used by ranchers, miners, and loggers, and those who believe preservation of wilderness and animals is more important. In an effort to gain additional public support and educate those who opposed reintroduction plans, Askins traveled to towns and cities all around the West. During her presentations and conferences she met not only with those who already supported her, but also with ranchers and others who regarded wolves as threats to their livestock. Some of these people came to view her as their enemy; leaders of powerful ranching and agricultural organizations claimed that she did not understand the true nature of the wolf, and she was soon hit by a wave of hate mail and obscene phone calls.

Askins did not let the setbacks and angry words get to her, though. One Fish and Wildlife Service official called her "one of the most dedicated

people I've ever run into. . . . She gets knocked down, gets up, cleans the dirt out of her ears, bats her big blue eyes, and goes on. I'm impressed that she hasn't lost her enthusiasm." For her part, Askins said that "I live in the West. These people are my neighbors and my friends. I understand what they're going through. So our efforts have been to try to create a solution that protects wolves as well as people."

Askins and her allies in the Wolf Fund were unable to convince all foes of wolf reintroduction that the idea was a good one. But she galvanized public support behind the initiative, and even some ranchers admitted that the efforts of Askins and others like her had made them reassess the situation. "I was real radical on the issue initially," recalled one rancher in *Audubon*. "But Renee and thousands of other people have convinced me that many people's lives would be improved by hearing the howl of a wolf." Another rancher pointed out that "the myth of the wolf has been handed down among ranchers for generations. But we live with other predators like coyotes and we don't have many problems. People fear the symbolism of the wolf more than they fear the animal itself. Renee is helping people understand that."

THE ARGUMENT FOR WOLVES

Indeed, Askins made a special effort to address the concerns of ranchers who worried about the impact of wolves on their livestock. She freely admitted that wolves would kill the occasional sheep or cow, but she also contended that "even if federal specialists have wildly underestimated the number of cows and sheep that wolves would kill in the Yellowstone and central Idaho areas, the actual total would be much smaller than the number that die each year in the state of Montana alone because of storms, dogs, and bovine ineptitude. In fact, the number of wolf-caused sheep deaths would have to be almost 30 times higher than predicted before it matched the number of Montana sheep that starved to death in 1993 because they rolled over onto their backs and were unable to get up."

Askins remained philosophical about those who opposed the Wolf Fund. "If I were a rancher I probably would not want wolves returned to the West," she once said. "If I faced the conditions that ranchers face in the West—falling stock prices, rising taxes, prolonged drought, and a nation that is eating less beef and wearing more synthetics—I would not want to add wolves to my woes. If I were a rancher in Montana, Idaho, or Wyoming in 1995, watching my neighbors give up and my way of life fade away, I would be afraid and I would be angry. I would want to blame something, to fight something, even kill something. The wolf is an ideal target: it is tangible, it is blamable, and it is real. Or is it? . . . Wolves aren't the cause of the changes occurring in the West any more than the rooster's crow is the cause of the sun's rising, but they have become the means by which ranchers can voice their concern about what's happening around them. Ranchers deserve our compassion and our concern. Whether the threat of wolves is imagined or actual, the ranchers' fear and anger are real. I honor that. However, it is my job, as a scientist and an advocate, to distinguish fact from fiction and purpose from perception."

Month after month, Askins worked for her cause, never losing sight of the final goal. "The rightness of this project is irrefutable. Wolves belong in Yellowstone," she claimed. "It is the world's oldest national park, and it has every plant and animal species that existed when Europeans hit the shores—except wolves. Yellowstone is the largest temperate ecosystem in the world, a World Biosphere Reserve. Its management techniques inform and guide parks through the world. It should be a model." Askins also argued that there were spiritual as well as scientific benefits to returning wolves to Yellowstone. "It is an act of giving back, a realigning, a recognition that we make ecological and ethical mistakes and learn from them, and what we learn can inform our actions. Thus, reintroducing wolves to Yellowstone is a symbolic act just as exterminating wolves from the West was a symbolic act. . . . Can't we have one place in America that is wild?"

WOLVES RETURN TO YELLOWSTONE

By 1993 the work of the Wolf Fund appeared to be drawing to a close. The U.S. Fish and Wildlife Service announced that plans to reintroduce wolves into Yellowstone and a region of the central Idaho wilderness were being made. Opponents of the plan were outraged—*Outside* magazine commented that "the hysteria that has always accompanied the subject of wolves reached new plateaus of lunacy" during this time—but it appeared that Askins and her allies had won. Environmentalists who were familiar with Askins praised her efforts. Noted wildlife biologist George Schaller called Askins's actions "conservation at its most basic and its best, done by a very dedicated person with a single goal," and writer Terry Tempest Williams proclaimed that "if the recovery of the wolf to Yellowstone is at the heart of saving our nation's most beloved national park, then Renee Askins is the heartbeat."

In January 1995, though, a final roadblock to reintroduction was constructed. Only weeks before 14 wolves were to be released into Yellowstone's wilderness (15 wolves had already been released in Idaho), two U.S. representatives led a successful battle to call legislative hearings on the plan before the U.S. House Committee on Resources. Askins traveled to Washington, D.C., to testify before the committee.

During her testimony Askins pointed out that both supporters and opponents of wolves sometimes misrepresented the facts. "Both environmentalists and ranchers have used exaggerated rhetoric to alarm constituents. . . . The tragedy is that while the armies fight their wars, the rest of America stands by, confused, uncertain, and unaware that something they care about might be at stake. The truth, as always, lies somewhere in the middle. Wolves are not killing machines that deserve hideous deaths; neither are they cuddly creatures needing tender, righteous protection. Wolves survive by killing; they have an extraordinary and complex social system; they are smart, strong, and, at the core, consummate predators. Restoring wolves will not rescue us from our economic or ecological troubles, but neither will their presence contribute to them. . . . Our attitudes toward wolves and our treatment of them cut to the very marrow of how we view our relationship to the natural world. Is wolf recovery loss or enrichment? Relinquishing or sharing? Wolves mean something to everyone. But in the end, wolves are only wolves. The real issue is one of making room, and there is still a little room in the West—room for hunters, for environmentalists, for ranchers, and for wolves."

After the hearings were over, the release of gray wolves into Yellowstone National Park went ahead as planned. On March 31, 1995, the wolves were released from their cages. As the lean gray forms disappeared into the forests and canyons of the park, Askins announced that, as promised, she was dissolving the Wolf Fund, for its mission had been achieved. Askins and the others who fought to place wolves back into Yellowstone know that the creatures face many challenges. Many ranchers in the Yellowstone region insist that they will shoot any wolf that strays onto their land, and opponents of the reintroduction effort remain very angry about the whole issue. But as Hampton Sides remarked in *Outside* in 1995, "for now, a phantom has become a fact. And there is a welcome new sound in the American Rockies: howling."

HOME AND FAMILY

Askins has lived for a number of years with folksinger Tom Rush, who helped her on Wolf Fund projects between concert performances. "I fell for her instantaneously," he admitted. "It's kind of like flying saucers. I don't believe in things like that happening, but it did." The couple live in a log cabin in Wyoming that looks out on the Grand Tetons.

FURTHER READING

BOOKS

Lopez, Barry. *Of Wolves and Men,* 1978
McIntyre, Rick. *A Society of Wolves: National Parks and the Battle over the Wolf,* 1993

PERIODICALS

Audubon, July-Aug. 1992, p.38
Economist, Jan. 7, 1995, p.A23
Harper's, Apr. 1995, p.15
Harper's Bazaar, Mar. 1994, p.322
Outside, Apr. 1995, p.106
Parade, May 13, 1990, p.16
People, Sep. 21, 1992, p.133

ADDRESS

Yellowstone Gray Wolf Project
P.O. Box 168
Yellowstone National Park, WY 82190

WORLD WIDE WEB SITE

http://www.pbs.org/ap/cause.html

David Brower   1912-
American Environmental Activist and
Writer
Founder of Earth Island Institute,
Friends of the Earth, and League of
Conservation Voters

BIRTH

David Ross Brower was born in Berkeley, California, on July
1, 1912. He was the third of four children born to Ross J. and
Mary Grace (Barlow) Brower. During David Brower's early
childhood, his father worked as an instructor in mechanical
drawing at the University of California, but he lost his job

when David was about eight. Luckily, Ross Brower owned two small apartment buildings in the area, and the family was able to get by on the revenue generated by these rental properties.

YOUTH

As a child, Brower became fascinated with the mighty railroad locomotives that ran past his family's home. "My earliest memory is of my brother, three years old, standing in his bed, silhouetted against the headlight of an oncoming railroad locomotive as it roared past our bedroom," Brower recalled. "I was six months old. Whoever doesn't believe this is invited to disprove it." His interest in railroads remained strong as he grew older, but other passions gradually began to get his attention as well.

Brower enjoyed playing the piano, which his mother had taught him to play, and he also found himself increasingly drawn to the rolling hills and lush forests that lay just outside his family's home. Armed with an old bicycle and a topographical map that showed the area's rivers, valleys, and hills, Brower roamed the countryside after completing his chores, seeking out butterflies and other wildlife. His parents also took the family on vacations deep into the Sierra Nevada (a mountain range in northern California), and Brower's eyes lit up at the sight of the towering peaks around him.

When Brower was eight years old, his mother was struck blind by an inoperable brain tumor. But she was determined that her blindness would not rob her of her enjoyment of the outdoors. Even though he was still a youngster, Brower volunteered to serve as her guide on her long walks. "You don't take your eyes for granted if you grew up with a mother who lost her sight when you were eight," he wrote. "You begin not only to look more carefully for yourself, but also to look for her, to see for her what she once saw and loved, to make your description of what you see for her as real as you can, and to find your reward in her response as she couples your words with what she remembers from when light meant something to her eyes."

Brower's early teen years were pretty tough. When he was a baby, he had fallen and severely hurt his mouth; he had major dental problems for a good part of his childhood as a result, and his front teeth did not grow in until he was 12. Other kids cruelly referred to him as the "toothless boob," and he became so self-conscious about his teeth that he rarely even smiled. Brower's social life was also hampered by his lack of ability at football and other sports that boys his age often played. As Brower recalled of one afternoon when he gave football a try, he "hadn't the foggiest idea how to pass a spiral or kick one. This to me was most dismal failure. Clearly I had spent too much time on music and butterflies."

Brower knew that his lack of athletic ability was regarded by his peers as a sure sign of his inferiority. "In the world of my contemporaries, if you were no good in sports you were no good period," Brower later wrote. But he made friends with a boy named Donald Madison Rubel, who set about teaching the skinny Brower how to play football and other games. They became close friends, and Brower began to gain more friends as he gained confidence in himself. Looking back on those days, Brower wrote that "Don's letting me share his world, and bringing out the athletic ability I would never otherwise have found, did something for me that nothing else did."

Brower was relieved that he no longer embarrassed himself when playing sports, but football and baseball and other activities never came close to replacing hiking, camping, and climbing in his heart. He sought out summer jobs that would allow him to spend his days outdoors, and by the time he was 17 he was guiding other hikers through the rugged Sierra Nevada. He also learned how to mountain climb around this time, and he soon spent many of his free hours climbing the cliffs of the Sierra Nevada.

EDUCATION

After graduating from Berkeley High School in 1928 at age 16, Brower enrolled at the University of California at Berkeley. He attended classes into his sophomore year, when he dropped out of school and took several clerical positions. "Yes, there was the Great Depression and there was no money in the family and I had to work. That's an excuse," Brower later wrote. "I started in January instead of with my friends in August. That's an excuse. I didn't like my major, entomology [the study of insects], but no courses were available in January anyway. I passed the Subject A English test [with an entomological essay] but failed the agility test, much to my embarrassment. That's no excuse, but it probably had more to do with my dropping out than the others. Let's not talk about it."

Looking back on his abbreviated college career, Brower remarked that his wife "periodically tries to make me feel better about my academic shortcomings. She knows no other sophomore dropout who has nine honorary degrees. She tells me that I have been able to do many of the things I have done because I didn't get enough education to know that they were impossible. And I occasionally say that I am a graduate of the University of the Colorado River. But I still didn't finish college, and I wish I had."

CAREER HIGHLIGHTS

After leaving college, Brower spent as much time as he could climbing and backpacking in the Sierra Nevada. Accompanied by only one or two friends on many of these trips, Brower sometimes disappeared for weeks at a time. He worked hard at his climbing skills during this period, and he was soon a fine mountaineer. In fact, Brower has been credited with 70 first ascents of various peaks, the vast majority of them in the Sierra Nevada range. "The rapture Brower experienced there transported him to a mystic state," said Marc Reisner in *Cadillac Desert*. "He had food and supplies cached all over the place; he could return to one weeks after laying it in and it would still be there. Like his hero John Muir [the conservationist who founded the Sierra Club], Brower grew intimate with vast proportions of that range."

THE SIERRA CLUB

After returning from one of these trips in 1933, Brower joined the Sierra Club. The conservation organization, which had been in existence since 1892, had been a big factor in preserving the Yosemite, Glacier, and Mt. Ranier National Parks. Brower emerged as one of the organization's hiking trip leaders, and his personality blossomed out in the mountains. "Once in the company of people who shared his devotion to alpine country, to climbing and skiing and waxing theological about the meaning of nature, Brower grew steadily more self-confident," said Russell Martin in *A Story That Sounds Like a Dam*.

In 1935 Brower secured a job with the Park Service at Yosemite National Park, and he also maintained his ties to the Sierra Club. He became an editor for the organization's *Sierra Club Bulletin* and established a friendship with fellow club member Ansel Adams, a famous nature photographer. Adams "changed my life," Brower later said. "His knowledge of photography and what could be done with it shaped everything I was going to do forever after." Indeed, Adams's photographs later inspired Brower to launch a publishing branch of the Sierra Club that would become renowned for its beautiful books on the wilderness.

In 1941 Brower took an editorial position at the University of California Press, where he met Anne Hus. They were married in 1943, the same year that Brower was sent overseas as part of the U.S. Army's Tenth Mountain Division. World War II was in full swing by this time, and Brower, who had enlisted in October 1942, had already been teaching soldiers about mountain climbing for several months. Stationed in the rugged Appennine Mountains of Italy, Brower's division took part in a number of battles, including a 1945 clash with German troops at Monte Torraccia. "That was the biggest battle I was in," he recalled. "We were still fighting three days after the war had ended because we didn't know it was over."

After returning to California, Brower resumed his position at the University of California Press. He continued to work for the Sierra Club, though, both as an editor for the *Sierra Club Bulletin* and a member of its board of directors. In 1952 he was named to lead the organization as its executive director. His energy and passion soon transformed the Sierra Club, which had drifted away from activism over the years, into a powerful force for environmental protection.

ENVIRONMENTAL BATTLES

In the aftermath of World War II, growing communities in the American West clamored for increased electricity and water, and the U.S. Bureau of Reclamation drew up plans to build dams on some rivers to provide these resources. But some of these proposed dams were targeted for beautiful wilderness areas, and Brower galvanized the Sierra Club into action against the most controversial of these proposals.

Utilizing the Sierra Club's growing publishing arm, full-age ads in newspapers such as the *New York Times*, research studies, and his own powers of persuasion, Brower launched an effective defense against assaults on two spectacular areas of American wilderness, Dinosaur National Monument in Colorado and Grand Canyon National Park in Arizona. Susan Zakin pointed out in *Coyotes and Town Dogs* that "letter writing, wilderness outings, dazzling congressional testimony, and full-page ads would become standard issue for hotshot environmental groups in the seventies and eighties. But before the Dinosaur fight, they had never been used on a mass political scale." Brower himself offered an eloquent defense of the region: "Under the proposed plan, the pinon pines, the Douglas firs, the maples and cottonwoods, the grasses and other flora that line the bank, the green living things that shine in the sun against the rich colors of the cliffs—these would all go. The river, its surge and its sound, the living sculptor of this place, would be silent forever, and all the fascination of its movement and the fun of riding it, quietly gliding through these cathedral corridors of stone—all done in for good."

Led by Brower, American environmentalists were able to save the canyons of Dinosaur National Monument, but they had little time to enjoy their victory. The dambuilders had targeted Grand Canyon National Park as well, and Brower knew that if the Grand Canyon—regarded by many as the crown jewel of America's national park system—fell to business interests, then the country's entire national park system would be endangered. The battle to save the Grand Canyon spanned 16 years, from 1952 to 1968, and Brower was in the thick of it the whole time. The Sierra Club waged a fierce publicity campaign to inform the public of the threat, and their efforts eventually paid off. In one newspaper ad, the organization cautioned Americans to "remember, with all the complexities of Washington politics and Arizona politics, and the ins and outs of committees and procedures, there is only one simple, incredible issue here: This time it's the Grand Canyon they want to flood. *The Grand Canyon.*"

In 1968 the dambuilders finally gave up the fight. The Grand Canyon was safe. Brower and the growing environmental movement posted other victories as well during the 1950s and 1960s. Looking back on that period of his life, Brower acknowledged that "we had a few more successes along the way — Point Reyes National Seashore, Fire Island, Cape Cod, Redwood National Park, North Cascades, the national wilderness system — some big wins." But he has had regrets as well. Brower freely admits that he remains haunted by the role he played in the damming of southern Utah's Glen Canyon. "Glen Canyon died in 1963 and I was partly responsible for its death," he wrote in the foreword to *The Place No One Knew*, a book of photographs that captured the canyon in its final days.

THE PLACE NO ONE KNEW: GLEN CANYON

As part of the deal that saved Dinosaur National Monument, Brower and the Sierra Club agreed to let a dam be built at Glen Canyon, an alternate site that few people had ever visited. Several months later, in the spring of 1957, Brower took his family on a rafting trip through the Glen Canyon area, and he was dazzled by the beauty of the place. He later wrote that the canyon was washed in its "own magic light, ricocheting from cliff to cliff, seeming to be independent of the thin arcs of sky we would occasionally see." A few years later, though, Glen Canyon was gone, its towering side canyons lost forever under the waters of the dammed up Colorado River. More than 30 years later, Brower still expresses sorrow about his role in the affair: "Never give up what you haven't seen. . . . And don't expect politicians, even good ones, to do the job for you. Politicians are like weather vanes. Our job [as environmentalists] is to make the wind blow."

CLASHES WITHIN THE SIERRA CLUB

By 1969 Brower was widely regarded as America's leading environmentalist. Around this time he came to be known as the "Archdruid" in recognition of his stature (according to Irish mythology, a druid was a type of magician who haunted the woods). But his relations with other Sierra Club leaders were falling apart. Critics said that Brower had become arrogant, and that he ignored those who disagreed with him. Even some of his friends, like Ansel Adams and writer Wallace Stegner, felt that Brower's personality had changed. Many members of the Sierra Club also worried that the organization's financial situation had deteriorated badly under Brower.

The Sierra Club had become a noted publisher of beautiful nature-oriented books by this time, but many of its publishing projects were very expensive. Club members had become increasingly concerned that Brower was endangering the group's financial health because of his heavy spending on books and other projects. Ansel Adams later acknowledged that Brower "intensely believed in what he did, but he acted with complete disregard for financial realities." Relations between Brower and the organization's board became so bad that he was finally fired, even though he had dramatically increased the club's membership (from 7,000 to 77,000) and its clout. "I think the real reason I was fired in 1969," said Brower, "was my opposition to developing nuclear power at Diablo Canyon in California. Until that moment, my other faults, which were beyond number, were tolerated, even forgiven." Indeed, many environmentalists of that time viewed nuclear power as a promising source of

nonpolluting energy, so Brower's unyielding opposition to the plant no doubt angered some of the organization's leaders.

Brower's dismissal from the Sierra Club did not affect his passion for wilderness conservation, though. He quickly launched three new environmental organizations: Friends of the Earth, the League of Conservation Voters (originally a subsidiary arm of the Friends of the Earth), and the John Muir Institute for Environmental Studies. Friends of the Earth was a politically active group that lobbied the government for earth-friendly legislation. The group also sponsored Earth Day, which was intended to remind citizens of their responsibilities toward the planet. The League of Conservation Voters was founded to keep voters informed about political candidates' stands on environmental issues, while the John Muir Institute was a nonprofit organization geared toward scientific research and education.

CONTINUING CONSERVATION WORK

During the 1970s Brower remained an active and eloquent defender of wilderness. Friends of the Earth and the Sierra Club worked on the same side of many issues, too, and Brower and the Sierra Club soon patched up their differences. Both parties seemed to recognize that whatever their problems, they were ultimately united in their concern for the environment. In 1972, only three years after he was fired, Brower was named an honorary vice president of the Sierra Club. Five years later he was given the club's highest award, the John Muir Award, in recognition of his conservation efforts.

By the early 1980s Friends of the Earth was an important part of the international conservation community. But internal clashes with his staff once again began to hurt Brower's position, and he eventually left the group. He promptly established a new organization called the Earth Island Institute. "Earth Island was even more innovative," wrote Susan Zakin. "The small groups that functioned under its umbrella were at the cutting edge of the mainstream environmental movement in the 1980s." Indeed, Earth Island's International Marine Mammal Project led the fight to protect dolphins from deadly tuna fishing practices around the world, and the organization has been a leader in recruiting minorities into the environmental movement.

In the mid-1990s Brower remains an influential and important member of America's environmental community. Still an active member of the Sierra Club, he led the successful campaign to make 23-year-old activist Adam Werbach (see entry in this volume of *Biography Today*) the organization's president in 1996, and he is heavily involved in the conservation efforts of Earth Island Institute and other environmental groups. He also remains one of America's most eloquent defenders of the wilderness, both in his books and in the many speeches that he gives across the country. And he continues to practice what he preaches: his 1995 book *Let the Mountains Talk, Let the Rivers Run* was the first book ever published on "tree-free" paper made from kenaf, a variety of flower.

ENVIRONMENTAL VIEWS

Brower has repeatedly cautioned that even though measures have been taken to protect the environment over the past few decades, many threats remain. He warns that such factors as overpopulation, corporate greed, global warming, and ozone depletion are all threats to the environment, and that people often do not recognize what they are doing to the wilderness until it is too late. "I do not blindly oppose progress," Brower once wrote. "I oppose blind progress." In talking about the logging of the world's forests, for instance, he acknowledges that the profession is the loggers' "livelihood" and "lifestyle," but says that "it is *our* future. I think . . . about all the wild beauty I saw for my mother, and the destruction of that beauty I've seen for myself. When this unsustainable orgy of cutting and running is finally over, the logger, like the buffalo hunter, like the whaler, will exist only in storybooks. I believe it will come true, and in your lifetime."

Brower is critical of environmental organizations, too, for he believes that too often they get bogged down by petty differences and jealousies. "The idea is not to claim turf. The idea is to save turf," he wrote. He also claims that too many environmental groups compromise with the world's polluters. "I'm giving all of them rather low grades," he said in 1994, "because they are not bold enough, and this planet is a beautiful-enough place to be bold about it when you want to protect it."

Still, Brower remains optimistic that wilderness lands can be saved if Americans adopt a conservation philosophy that he calls CPR: Conservation, Preservation, and Restoration. "It's exciting to change the world," he said. "I've had some big ideas in my life. I've made some things happen. I've stopped some misguided people from trashing the Earth. But the idea I believe I will be checking out on is restoration, although I have no intention of checking out any sooner than necessary. I've grown very fond of this planet. I want to help save a taste of paradise for our children. . . . Let us begin. Let us restore the Earth. Let the mountains talk, and the rivers run. Once more, and forever."

LEGACY

Brower is universally regarded as one of the greatest of America's defenders of wilderness and the environment. Author Hazel Henderson said that "David Brower is quite simply a unique figure in the environmental movement. I marvel at his bedrock integrity and clarity of vision and purpose." Ansel Adams agreed, writing that "the earth is a better place because of this resolute crusader for the environment."

Indeed, Brower's passion has played an important part in establishing protection and safeguards for America's natural resources over the past four decades. As David Kupfer wrote in *The Progressive*, "his life has been exceptional, inspiring, exciting, turbulent on occasion, and even a little crazy. In his own crusading manner, he has built a fire under the environmental community and kept it stoked for decades. By both his example and his spirit, he is constantly reminding us that [as German poet Johann von Goethe put it] 'boldness has genius, power, and magic in it.'"

MARRIAGE AND FAMILY

Brower married Anne Hus on May 1, 1943. They had four children — Kenneth, Robert, Barbara, and John — whom they raised in the Berkeley home where Brower and his wife continue to live. The children recalled that although they had little exposure to formal religion while they were growing up, their father gave them a great appreciation for the natural wonders around them. Brower himself once said that "my church is the outdoors. John Muir said God's cathedrals were the mountains and the forests, and I buy that." Despite their busy schedules, David and Anne Brower continue to escape into the Sierra Nevada whenever they can.

Once there, they roam far away from the crowds of tourists that push through the mountains. "When people say Yosemite is crowded, they don't realize that all you have to do is get off the trail," said Brower. "Anne and I like to go to places in the Sierra where there are no trails."

WRITINGS

Manual of Ski Mountaineering, 1942
The Meaning of Wilderness to Science, 1960
Wildlands in Our Civilization, 1964 (editor)
Not Man Apart: The Big Sur Coast, 1965 (editor)
Going Light — With Backpack or Burro, 1970
For Earth's Sake: The Life and Times of David Brower, 1990
Work in Progress, 1991
Let the Mountains Talk, Let the Rivers Run, 1995 (with Steve Chapple)

HONORS AND AWARDS

Bronze Star (U.S. Army): 1945
California Conservation Council Award: 1953
National Parks Association Award: 1956
Carey-Thomas Award: 1964
Paul Bartsch Award (Audubon Naturalist Society of Central Atlantic States): 1967
John Muir Award (Sierra Club): 1977
Golden Ark Award (Prince of Netherlands): 1979
Golden Gadfly Award (Media Alliance of San Francisco): 1984
Rose Award (World Environment Festival): 1986
Robert Marshall Award (Wilderness Society): 1994

FURTHER READING

BOOKS

Adams, Ansel. *Ansel Adams: An Autobiography,* 1985
Anker, Debby, and John de Graaf. *David Brower: Friend of the Earth,* 1993 (juvenile)
Brower, David R. *Environmental Activist, Publicist, and Prophet,* 1979 (interviews with Susan Schrepfer)
———. *For Earth's Sake: The Life and Times of David Brower,* 1991
———. *Let the Mountains Talk, Let the Rivers Run,* 1995 (with Steve Chapple)
Cohen, Michael P. *The History of the Sierra Club 1892-1970,* 1988
Fox, Stephen. *The American Conservation Movement: John Muir and His Legacy,* 1985
Martin, Russell. *A Story That Sounds Like a Dam: Glen Canyon and the Struggle for the Soul of the West,* 1989

McPhee, John. *Encounters with the Archdruid,* 1971
Porter, Eliot. *The Place No One Knew,* 1963
Reisner, Marc. *Cadillac Desert,* 1986
Who's Who in America, 1996
Zakin, Susan. *Coyotes and Town Dogs: Earth First! and the Environmental Movement,* 1993

PERIODICALS

America, Apr. 22, 1995, p.8
Buzzworm, July-Aug. 1993, p.31
National Geographic, June 1954, p.844
New York Times, Sep. 17, 1969, p.A21
The Progressive, May 1994, p.36
Sierra, Sep.-Oct. 1993, p.32
Sports Illustrated, Apr. 14, 1969, p.36
Whole Earth Review, Fall 1995, p.111

ADDRESS

Earth Island Institute
300 Broadway
San Francisco, CA 94133

WORLD WIDE WEB SITE

http://www.earthisland.org/ei

Rachel Carson 1907-1964
American Biologist and Writer
Author of *Silent Spring,* which Alerted
America to the Dangers of Pesticides

BIRTH

Rachel Louise Carson was born on May 27, 1907, in Springdale, Pennsylvania. Her father, Robert Warden Carson, worked at a local electric station, but he also spent time as an insurance agent and real estate agent. Her mother, Maria (McLean) Carson, was a schoolteacher for a while, but in keeping with the era, she gave up her job to be a homemaker after she was married. Rachel Carson was the youngest of three children. Her sister, Marian, was born in 1897, while her brother, Robert, Jr., was born two years later.

YOUTH

Carson grew up in Springdale, a small town about 15 miles north of Pittsburgh. She was not exactly poor as a child, but money was always tight. Although her family lived close to the big city, Carson became familiar with the world of nature at an early age. The family lived on a 65-acre lot that was dotted with woods and trickling springs, and wildlife was abundant in the area.

"I can remember no time when I wasn't interested in the out-of-doors and the whole world of nature," Carson later recalled. "Those interests, I know, I inherited from my mother and have always shared with her. I was rather a solitary child and spent a great deal of time in woods and beside streams, learning the birds and the insects and flowers." She also had pets throughout her childhood. She was quite devoted to the cats and dogs that followed her around the house and the yard, in part because they were often her only companions. Both her brother and sister were much older than she was, and the family's rural location made it difficult for her to find playmates.

Carson had a hard time making friends at school, too. She was very shy, and her mother often kept her at home whenever she heard that flus or colds were making the rounds at her school. Carson had been stricken with scarlet fever as a young child, and the illness prompted Maria Carson to be very cautious about keeping her healthy. Despite Carson's frequent absences from school, though, her education did not suffer. Her mother was an enthusiastic and talented tutor, and she made sure that Rachel did not fall behind.

Even as a youngster, Carson loved to read. Stories about animals particularly appealed to her, and as she grew older, she decided that she would be a writer. "I suppose I must have realized someone wrote the books and thought it would be fun to make up stories, too," she remarked. One day the Carson family received a letter from her brother, who had joined the U.S. Army Aviation Service (which later became the Air Force) during World War I. He included a story about a brave pilot whose plane had been hit by German gunfire, and his little sister was so inspired by the story that she decided to write an account of it herself.

Carson called the story "A Battle in the Clouds," and as soon as she had completed it, she mailed it to a children's magazine called *St. Nicholas*, which often published stories and poems written by young readers.

Carson's story was published several months later, and she even received a $10 award for her work. "I doubt that any royalty check of recent years has given me as great a joy as the notice of the award," she later said. "Perhaps that early experience of seeing my work in print played its part in fostering my childhood dream of becoming a writer."

EDUCATION

During her childhood and youth, Carson attended public schools in Springdale and New Kensington, a town just a few miles down the road. In 1925 she graduated from Parnassus Senior High School in New Kensington as one of its top students. Even the caption next to her photo in the high school yearbook was an acknowledgment of her academic achievements: "Rachel's like the mid-day sun/Always very bright/Never stops her studying/'Til she gets it right."

In 1925 an academic scholarship allowed Carson to begin taking classes at the Pennsylvania College for Women in Pittsburgh. Her classmates, many of whom came from wealthy families, recognized that Carson was very bright, but she never really fit into any social circles. One of her college classmates later reflected that Carson "wasn't anti-social. She just wasn't social. Being poor had some bearing on that. She didn't have the clothes or the extra things a girl needed at college then." Carson spent most of her time studying or writing, and she spent most of her weekends back at her parents' house in Springdale.

Carson originally planned to pursue her long-time interest in writing at college, but by her junior year she had become increasingly fascinated by biology and natural history. She decided to change her major to biology, even though many people at the time thought that women were not smart enough to take such challenging course work. Her classmates, her professors, and even the college president thought that her decision was a foolish one, but she remained calm in the face of all the second-guessing. "You ought to see the reactions I get [to the news]," she wrote to a friend. "I've gotten bawled out and called all sorts of blankety-blank names so much that it's beginning to get monotonous. That's all from the other girls, of course."

In 1929 Carson graduated with a major in biology and a minor in English. Her high grades attracted the attention of officials at the prestigious Johns Hopkins University in Baltimore, and they offered her a $200 scholarship for graduate school. First, though, she spent a summer studying at the Marine Biological Laboratory at Woods Hole, Massachusetts. The laboratory, which was a very well-known marine research facility, had a tremendous impact on Carson.

Long fascinated by the ocean and its magnificent variety of marine life, Carson finally had the opportunity to investigate the sea for herself. She spent hours exploring the Pacific Ocean shoreline and tidal pools, studying the creatures that she saw there. When she was not out in the ocean air, she could usually be found poring through the facility's extensive library. Before she knew it, the summer was over and it was time to begin her marine biology studies at Johns Hopkins. But she never forgot those first weeks at Woods Hole, and she returned to the facility on a number of occasions over the coming years.

In 1931 Carson joined the zoology staff at the University of Maryland, and a year later she received her master's degree from Johns Hopkins. She stayed at Maryland until 1936, when she was offered a position as an aquatic biologist with the U.S. Bureau of Fisheries in Washington, D.C. She had first come to the attention of the bureau several months earlier, when she had been hired to compose short scripts on ocean life for its radio show. Once she was hired on a full-time basis, Carson was delighted to find that her work allowed her to combine her love of science and writing. Up to that point, Carson later said, "I thought I had to be one or the other; it never occurred to me, or apparently to anyone else, that I could combine the two careers."

CAREER HIGHLIGHTS

In 1937 Carson wrote an essay titled "Undersea," in which she offered an evocative glimpse into the lives of the creatures that roamed far below the ocean's surface. Her supervisor encouraged her to send the piece to the *Atlantic Monthly,* one of the nation's leading magazines. After a few months of indecision, she sent it to the magazine, but she did not have very high hopes that it would be accepted. After all, she was totally unknown, and the *Atlantic Monthly* was able to choose from the efforts of many established writers. She was shocked, then, when the magazine accepted her article and published it in its September 1937 issue.

A short time later, recalled Carson, "Quincy Howe, then editor for Simon and Schuster, wrote to ask why I didn't do a book. So did Hendrik Willem van Loon [author of a bestselling book called *The Story of Mankind*]. My mail had never contained anything so exciting as his first letter." Encouraged by the kind words of Howe, van Loon, and many other *Atlantic* readers, she set about to write a full-length book about the amazing variety of sea life that existed on the planet.

UNDER THE SEA-WIND

The topic that Carson chose for her first book involved a great deal of hard research, and the writing went slowly. But after more than three years of

studying, writing, revising, and editing, the manuscript was completed. The volume, which she titled *Under the Sea-Wind* (1942), was a lovely narrative that won praise from many critics. Carson was grateful for the kind words, for she had poured her heart into the book. "*Under the Sea-Wind* was written to make the sea and its life as vivid a reality for those who may read the book as it has become for me during the past decade," she wrote. "It was written, moreover, out of the deep conviction that the life of the sea is worth knowing. To stand at the edge of the sea, to sense the ebb and the flow of the tides, to feel the breath of a mist moving over a great salt marsh, to watch the flight of shore birds that have swept up and down the surf lines of the continents for untold thousands of years . . . is to have knowledge of things that are as nearly eternal as any earthly life can be. These things . . . continue year in, year out, through the centuries and the ages, while man's kingdoms rise and fall."

Although it was praised by critics, the book did not sell well. The poor sales of *Under the Sea- Wind* disappointed Carson, and she vowed that she would never write another full-length book. "I am convinced that writing a book is a very poor gamble financially," she explained to a friend.

Besides, her responsibilities at work were taking up a great deal of time. By this time, she had risen to a supervisor position in the Fish and Wildlife Service, which had been formed in 1940 by a merger of the Bureau of Fisheries and the Bureau of Biological Survey. One colleague recalled that "she had no patience with dishonesty or shirking in any form and she didn't appreciate anybody being dumb. But she always showed much more tolerance for a dull-minded person who was honest than for a bright one who wasn't. She was just so doggone good she couldn't see why other people couldn't try to be the same. She had standards, high ones." In 1949 she was promoted yet again, to editor-in-chief of Fish and Wildlife's publishing concerns.

The late 1940s also marked the rebirth of Carson's book-writing career. Despite her earlier decision to avoid writing books, she found herself drawn to the idea of composing another volume about the ocean. Many insights into ocean life had been made during the 1940s, and she hoped to incorporate these findings into the book that was taking shape in her mind.

After more than two years of research and writing, Carson's second book—*The Sea Around Us*—was published in 1952. The book, which was arranged as a sort of guide to the ocean's changes, both over time and at its various depths, proved to be an enormous critical and popular success. Reviewers marveled over her ability to meld science and lyrical writing so seamlessly, while the publication of several of its chapters in the *New Yorker* helped push it onto the bestseller lists. When the book was given the National Book Award, Carson knew that she would no longer have to do her writing in her spare time. Armed with a number of grants and fellowships from various foundations, she quit her job and turned to writing on a full-time basis.

Carson's third book, *The Edge of the Sea,* was published in 1956. A book devoted to explaining the creatures that made their home in the world's oceans, it was warmly received as well. By this time she was fairly well-known in the literary community, but she was hardly famous. But two years later she received a letter from a friend that changed her life forever.

GROWING CONCERN ABOUT PESTICIDES

In January 1958 Carson received a letter from Olga Owens Huckins, a friend who, with her husband, had created a bird sanctuary on their property. The birds had thrived there until a plane spraying the pesticide DDT (dichlorodiphenyl trichloroethane) had passed overhead. DDT was commonly used at that time across much of America to kill mosquitos and other insects. Soon after the spraying, Huckins found that the birds on their land were dying in bunches. "All of these birds died horribly, and in the same way," wrote Huckins. "Their bills were gaping open, and their splayed claws were drawn up to their breasts in agony."

The letter seemed to confirm some of Carson's worst fears about DDT. For years she had been tracking reports about pesticide use in newspapers and government documents with growing uneasiness. After receiving Huckins's letter, she began digging deeper. Her research heightened her concerns about the possible dangers that pesticide-spraying practices posed to people, animals, and the country's forests and rivers. Alarmed at the information that she was uncovering, she tried to write magazine articles that would spell out her concerns. All the magazines she contacted turned her down, though, so she set out to write a book on the subject. "The more I learned about the use of pesticides the more appalled I became," she said. "What I discovered was that everything which meant most to me as a naturalist was being threatened, and that nothing I could do would be more important. However, I wanted to do more than merely express concern: I wanted to demonstrate that that concern was well founded." Four years later, in 1962, *Silent Spring* was published. More than 30 years later, it is still regarded by many people as the book that launched a revolution in environmental protection in America.

SILENT SPRING

Carson battled through a number of serious ailments to produce *Silent Spring*. In the spring of 1960 she discovered that she had breast cancer, and the radiation treatments that followed weakened her terribly. Other illnesses, including an eye infection that blinded her for a few weeks, also presented obstacles, but she fought through all of them. She was determined to complete the book, which she had come to think of as her most important work. Finally, after countless hours of sifting through research, studying lab tests, and revising her words, *Silent Spring* was complete.

Shortly before the book itself was published, the *New Yorker* arranged to publish excerpts from *Silent Spring*. Writing to a friend, Carson described how she felt when she learned how impressed the magazine's editor had been with her work: "Suddenly the tension of four years was broken and I let the tears come. I think I let you see last summer what my deeper feelings are about this when I said I could never again listen happily to a thrush song if I had not done all I could. And last night the thoughts of all the birds and other creatures and all the loveliness that is in nature came to me with such a surge of deep happiness, that now I had done what I could — I had been able to complete it — now it had a life of its own."

When *Silent Spring* was published in September 1962, it immediately became one of the most controversial books ever published. Meticulously researched and powerfully written, *Silent Spring* bluntly warned us that the planet was being poisoned by the indiscriminate use of pesticides. Manufacturers of DDT, aldrin, chlordane, and other highly toxic chemicals that were discussed in the book savagely attacked her, as she knew they would. "When the attack did come, it was probably as bitter and unscrupulous as anything of the sort since the publication of Charles Darwin's *Origin of Species* a century before," wrote Paul Brooks, Carson's long-time editor. "Hundreds of thousands of dollars were spent by the chemical industry in an attempt to discredit the book and to malign the author—she was described as an ignorant and hysterical woman who wanted to turn the earth over to the insects." *Time, Newsweek,* and other leading magazines initially dismissed the book, saying that it was riddled with errors and unprofessional emotionalism.

Others, though, rushed to Carson's defense. Leading scientists found that her research was impeccable and her arguments persuasive, while many editors and columnists called for further investigation into her charges. The American public was alarmed as well, and thousands of letters poured into government agencies demanding further research into the dangers of pesticides. Even President John F. Kennedy indicated that he found many of Carson's warnings to be worth studying, and he established a commission to look into the issue.

Criticism of *Silent Spring* subsided after government investigators endorsed her research and data, and other scientists soon joined Carson in warning about the potential hazards of DDT and other pesticides. By the end of 1962 dozens of bills intended to curb pesticide use were introduced in state legislatures around the country. Carson had achieved what she had set out to do: make the American public aware of the poisons that threatened their very lives.

Carson's health continued to deteriorate, though. The cancer in her body was spreading, and the radiation treatments that she endured left her listless and weak. Numerous conservation awards and honors were bestowed upon her during the last months of her life, but she was often unable to attend the ceremonies that were held in her honor. On April 14, 1964, Carson died of cancer and heart disease. Five years later, the Coastal Maine Refuge, an area that looked out on the ocean that she loved so much, was renamed the Rachel Carson National Wildlife Refuge in her honor.

CARSON'S LEGACY

"Carson's warnings triggered a wave of environmental reforms that held back the day of reckoning she foresaw," wrote Gregg Easterbrook in *Newsweek.* Indeed, the publication of *Silent Spring* spurred a new awareness of the importance of environmental protection. Hundreds of state and federal laws designed to protect the environment are now in place, and such deadly pesticides as DDT, aldrin, and dieldrin have been banned. Government agencies, including the Environmental Protection Agency (EPA), have been formed as well to protect the country's natural resources.

In 1980 President Jimmy Carter posthumously awarded Carson the Presidential Medal of Freedom, the highest honor that an American civilian can attain. "Rachel Carson fed a spring of awareness across America and beyond," said Carter during the ceremony. "A biologist with a gentle, clear voice, she welcomed her audiences to her love of the sea, while with an equally clear, determined voice she warned Americans of the dangers human beings pose for their own environment. Always concerned, always eloquent, she created a tide of environmental consciousness that has not ebbed." Indeed, more than 30 years after her death, Carson remains one of the true giants of the American environmental movement.

HOME AND FAMILY

Carson never married, but she did help to raise other members of the Carson family. When her divorced sister died in 1937, Carson and her mother took responsibility for her two young daughters, Marjorie and Virginia. Virginia later recalled that her aunt "was more like an older sister; she was a lot of fun, and certainly made a happy home for us." Nearly 20 years later, Carson adopted Marjorie's son Roger, who had lost his father at an early age, after Marjorie died of pneumonia.

WRITINGS

Under the Sea-Wind, 1942
The Sea Around Us, 1951
The Edge of the Sea, 1955
Silent Spring, 1962
The Sense of Wonder, 1965

HONORS AND AWARDS

Eugene F. Saxton Memorial Fellowship: 1949
George Westinghouse Foundation Award (for outstanding science writing): 1950
Guggenheim Fellowship: 1951
National Book Award: 1951, for *The Sea Around Us*
Frances Hutchinson Medal (Garden Club of America): 1952
John Burroughs Medal: 1952
National Book Award: 1952
Achievement Award (American Association of University Women): 1956
Audubon Medal (National Audubon Society): 1963

Conservation Award (Isaak Walton League of America): 1963
Conservationist of the Year (National Wildlife Federation): 1963
Constance Lindsay Skinner Award (Women's National Book Association):
    1963
Cullum Medal (American Geographical Society): 1963
Election to American Academy of Arts and Letters: 1963
New England Outdoor Writers Association Award: 1963
Schweitzer Medal (Animal Welfare Institute): 1963
Presidential Medal of Freedom: 1980

FURTHER READING

BOOKS

Benet's Reader's Encyclopedia of American Literature, 1991
Briggs, Shirley A. *Silent Spring—The View from 1987,* 1987
Brooks, Paul. *The House of Life: Rachel Carson at Work,* 1972
Carson, Rachel. *Silent Spring,* 1962
Columbia Encyclopedia, 1993
Encyclopedia Britannica, 1985
Faber, Doris, and Harold Faber. *Nature and the Environment,* 1991
Harlan, Judith. *Sounding the Alarm—A Biography of Rachel Carson,* 1989
Jezer, Marty. *Rachel Carson,* 1988 (juvenile)
Presnall, Judith Janda. *The Importance of Rachel Carson,* 1995
Ravage, Barbara. *Rachel Carson: Gentle Crusader,* 1997 (juvenile)
Sterling, Philip. *Sea and Earth: The Life of Rachel Carson,* 1970
Stwertka, Eve. *Rachel Carson,* 1991 (juvenile)
Wadsworth, Ginger. *Rachel Carson,* 1992 (juvenile)

PERIODICALS

Current Biography 1951
Field and Stream, Dec. 1995, p.55
New York Times, Apr. 15, 1964, p.A1
New York Times Book Review, Oct. 6, 1996, p.88
New Yorker, June 7, 1993, p.114
Newsweek, Nov. 28, 1994, p.72
Outdoor Life, Jan. 1993, p.54
Sierra, Sep./Oct. 1994, p.84

WORLD WIDE WEB SITES

http://www.sirius.com/~fitch/wells/carson/carson/.html
http://www.lm.com/~markt/rachel/carson.html

Marjory Stoneman Douglas   1890-
American Writer and Conservationist
Leader in Fight to Protect and Restore
Florida's Everglades

BIRTH

Marjory Stoneman Douglas was born on April 7, 1890, in
Minneapolis, Minnesota. Her father, Frank Bryant Stoneman,
was a businessman, attorney, and newspaper editor. Her
mother, Lillian Trefethen, was a concert violinist. Marjory was
their only child.

YOUTH

Douglas spent the first three years of her life in Minneapolis, where her father ran a building and loan business. After this business failed during the economic depression of 1893, the family moved to Providence, Rhode Island. Douglas's father, who had a new job selling oil, would often read to her in the evenings. One time, while listening to *Hiawatha*, Douglas became very upset when Hiawatha stripped the bark off of a birch tree to make a canoe. From that time on, her father made sure he skipped that part of the story.

At the age of four, Douglas made her first visit to the South. Her family rode a train to New Orleans, then took a ship across the Gulf of Mexico to Florida. Even as a little girl, Douglas thought Florida was a magical place. She always remembered the special quality of the sunlight, and the taste of an orange picked fresh off the tree.

When her father's oil business failed the following year, Douglas's family life took a sudden turn. Her mother left her father, packing up her things and moving with five-year-old Marjory to the Trefethen home in Taunton, Massachusetts. Though Douglas enjoyed living with her grandparents, she missed her father and was sad when it became clear that her parents' separation would be permanent. To make matters worse, her mother soon had a nervous breakdown and spent several months in a hospital. Douglas noted that her mother seemed less energetic and more fragile afterward.

Throughout her childhood, Douglas's favorite pastime was reading. She loved to sneak off to the quiet attic of her grandparents' house to spend hours in the company of her beloved books. "You couldn't drag me away from books or books away from me," she remembered. Douglas's grandmother encouraged her to take piano lessons, but she never enjoyed it. Since her whole family had great musical ability, she soon became discouraged by her comparative lack of talent and quit.

EDUCATION

Douglas attended the public schools in Taunton. She always loved school, excelling in every subject except math. She claimed that her young mind was like "a dried-out sponge, ready to absorb every kind of substance there is around." She especially enjoyed writing poems and stories, and she was thrilled when one of her submissions was published in the children's magazine *St. Nicholas*.

Although it was rare in those days for women to attend college, Douglas was given the opportunity by her Aunt Fanny, who offered to pay the tuition. She began taking classes at Wellesley College, a prestigious women's college near Boston, in the fall of 1908. Many of the courses she took there influenced her thinking later in life, including geology, geography, and social economics. During her junior year, Douglas had her first essay published in the college literary magazine. She also became active in the nationwide campaign to secure the right to vote for women. In 1910, she founded the Equal Suffrage League with some of her classmates to promote their views on the issue. The group remained active until 1920, when all American women were granted the right to vote by the 19th amendment to the Constitution. In her senior year, Douglas was named editor of the college yearbook.

Sadly, Douglas's mother was ill with cancer during most of this time. Douglas sent a postcard home to her every day for the four years she attended Wellesley, and visited whenever she could. Just a few weeks after Douglas graduated in the spring of 1912 with a bachelor's degree in English composition, her mother died.

CAREER HIGHLIGHTS

For the first few years after she graduated, Douglas worked in department stores in St. Louis, Missouri, and Newark, New Jersey. She never really enjoyed the work, however, and hoped to find something more suited to her interests and abilities. The chance she had been waiting for came in 1915. Her father, whom she had not seen in years, had moved to Florida and started a newspaper. Years after he sold it, this paper became the *Miami Herald*, which today is one of America's largest newspapers. Douglas moved to Miami, which at that time was a small town, and went to work for her father. At first she filled in as the society editor, writing columns about local parties and weddings, but before long she became a regular reporter. She also made a number of new friends—including her stepmother, Lilla—and enjoyed picnicking at the beach and swimming in the ocean.

In 1917, after the United States had entered World War II, the Navy sent a recruiting ship to Miami to encourage people to enlist in the Naval Reserves. Douglas received an assignment to go down to the docks and interview the first woman to enlist. Instead, she ended up volunteering herself. "Look, I got the story on the first woman to enlist," she told her father when she returned to the newspaper office. "It turned out to be me." Her Navy assignment was a disappointment, however, as she wound up at a desk job in Miami issuing boat licenses. She received an honorable discharge after a year and then joined the American Red Cross, hoping to make a bigger contribution to the war effort. Douglas was sent to Europe, where she worked with war refugees throughout France. After the war ended, she continued to tour war-torn Europe, visiting hospitals and bringing relief supplies to the people of the Balkans and Greece. Throughout her wartime service, Douglas wrote stories about her experiences that were reprinted in newspapers around the United States.

In 1920, Douglas returned home to become assistant editor of the *Miami Herald.* Much to her dismay, she found that the small town she had left was changing rapidly as a result of a post-war boom in building. Farmers, developers, and land speculators were buying up property on the outskirts of Miami with reckless abandon. Much of the land was covered with marshy wetlands, which they drained of water in order to build homes or plant crops. Douglas foresaw problems with this situation. What had once been a "delicate balance between nature and a small population," according to Douglas, was being destroyed by "hordes of men obsessed by a manic belief in millions to be made by gambling with the prices of land for which they knew or cared nothing."

Douglas wrote her own column in the paper about national and local affairs, and she frequently used it to speak out about the problems she saw in society. Over time, however, the pace at the paper became too hectic for her, and she started having disagreements with the publisher. She finally resigned from her job in 1924 in order to rest. She recovered by writing short stories, and before long one was accepted by the prominent national magazine *Saturday Evening Post.* Douglas received $500 for the story, which forced her skeptical family to believe that she could indeed make a living as an author.

Douglas used the money to buy some land and build her own house in Coconut Grove, a section of Miami known for its beautiful gardens and many artist residents. She continued writing and publishing stories in a variety of well-known magazines over the years, and her adopted home of Florida was central to much of her work. One of her most compelling pieces, "Plumes," tells the true story of Guy Bradley, a game warden who was murdered by bird poachers in the Everglades. In the early 1900s, thousands of Florida birds were killed by hunters for their valuable feathers, which were used to decorate hats. Bradley was shot when he tried to enforce a law against killing birds, and his murderers were later allowed to go free. Douglas's story provoked outrage around the country and raised public awareness of mismanagement of the Everglades.

THE EVERGLADES

Though many people think of the Everglades as a huge swamp, it is in fact a slow-moving river. Between 50 and 70 miles wide and an average of 6 inches deep, the water of the Everglades drops 2 to 3 inches per mile as it flows over 100 miles from Lake Okeechobee in south-central Florida to the Florida Bay on the southernmost tip of the peninsula. The unique Everglades ecosystem, which combines freshwater and saltwater, is home to 300 varieties of birds, 600 species of fish, and 40 types of indigenous plants. It provides habitat for wood storks, herons, kites, osprey, bald eagles, alligators and crocodiles, manatee and porpoises, otter, deer, and the endangered Florida panther.

The most common plant in the Everglades is sawgrass, which can grow up to 12 feet tall and gets its name from its razor-sharp edges. In some places, the Everglades seems to be an endless marsh of sawgrass. There are also thousands of islands, or hammocks, made of sand and limestone dotting the Everglades. Most hammocks are covered with a variety of tropical flowers and trees. Around the southern edge of the Everglades are dense forests of mangrove trees, which have long, twisted roots that are specially adapted to growing in the water.

Douglas became active in the fight to preserve the Everglades in 1928, when she joined the Tropical Everglades Park Association. The association was founded by Ernest Coe, a landscape architect who had become captivated by the unique biology of the Everglades. Coe and his organization worked to convince the federal government to preserve and protect the Everglades by designating the area as a national park. Many people were opposed to this idea, however. Some felt that the national park designation should be reserved for places with spectacular scenery—like Yosemite in California or the Grand Canyon in Arizona—rather than given to what they considered to be a vast swamp full of snakes and alligators. Others owned property in the area that they hoped to develop, and they knew that the national park designation would prevent them from doing so. Discussions about whether the Everglades should become a national park went on for many years.

RIVER OF GRASS

In 1942, Douglas was asked to write a book about the Miami River. Instead, she decided to write about the Everglades, which she called a "river of grass." During four years of research, she explored the area extensively in a canoe and on foot. She also spoke with many historians, bird experts, water experts, and ordinary people who lived in the area. "I don't know the names of half the people with whom I leaned on bridges or drank Cokes in trail stations or hailed from fishing docks or gossiped with in lonely houses, on hidden roads, on beaches or by solitary rivers or on the corners of crowded streets," she stated. The result was *The Everglades: River of Grass,* which was published in 1947 and quickly became a best-seller.

In her book, which has been called a "treasured classic of nature writing," Douglas described the Everglades, traced its history, and drew attention to the problems it faced. For example, in the book's final chapter, called "The Eleventh Hour," Douglas discussed the terrible results of early efforts to drain the Everglades and convert it to farm and residential land. Through the mid-1940s, as a vast system of dams and canals was built to drain water out of the area, hundreds of acres of sawgrass dried out and caught

on fire. "In a week in which the fires spread into the drying jungles, flashed across the firebreaks, the flames worked and smoldered deep into the roots and hearts of the beautiful old live oaks," Douglas wrote. "All the fine tropical trees of the jungle were eaten out. Birds, snakes, deer, small animals were caught in the flames. The delicate tree snails were burned, the orchids, the air plants, the ancient leather ferns, the butterflies. What had been unique and lovely and strange was a black monotony of destruction." In addition to the fires, the drainage of freshwater caused saltwater to flow into the region at a rate of between 250 and 1,000 feet per year, destroying crops and farmland and contaminating drinking water supplies.

Douglas's book helped draw national attention to what was happening in the Everglades. People in South Florida began organizing to protect their unique natural resource by attending meetings, writing letters, and signing petitions. Their actions began to show results almost immediately. After years of haggling, Everglades National Park was finally established in 1947, encompassing 1.5 million acres in the southern part of the Everglades. Before long, steps were taken to coordinate management of the entire ecosystem under a single board of engineers.

But while people had begun to take a greater interest in protecting the Everglades, the population of South Florida continued to grow year after year, placing ever-increasing demands on the region's natural resources. As Douglas explained, "The population increase has brought people to the state who don't know, or care, about the environment. This increase occurred upon a very fragile environment where there is a natural balance between fresh and salt water. The enormous population has completely upset that natural balance, and that is our great problem. If the people weren't here, we wouldn't have the problem with the environment—it's all a result of overpopulation, ignorance, stupidity, and a desire of some people to make a quick buck."

FRIENDS OF THE EVERGLADES

In the late 1960s, Miami's city planners started to discuss constructing a 39-square-mile airport in the Everglades. Douglas was outraged by this idea, realizing that the development would cause a major disruption in the flow of the river. In response, she founded an organization called Friends of the Everglades in 1969 to fight the airport proposal. Then 79 years old, she attracted a great deal of attention as she made public appearances all over Florida—usually wearing a flowery-print dress and straw hat—to inform people about the importance of preserving the Everglades. Thanks in part to her efforts, the airport was never built. Membership in Friends of the Everglades grew rapidly, topping 1,000 within two years. Douglas's vocal opinions were not popular with everyone, however. At one public hearing on the Everglades, someone in the back of the room shouted "Go home, Granny" during her remarks. Unfazed, Douglas replied, "You might as well sit down. I've got all night, and I'm used to the heat."

Threats to the Everglades continued to mount during the 1970s. One study found that the population of wading birds in the region had declined dramatically—from 2.5 million in 1870 to 250,000 in 1970, or a 90 percent decrease—due to habitat destruction and artificial changes in water levels. "The decline of birds has been one of the most tragic and visible signs of trouble in the Everglades," Douglas wrote. "Biologists note that birds can serve as excellent indicators of the quality of habitat—not just their own, but that of the humans who share the land. When the Everglades can no longer support the birds, the people will inevitably suffer, for the ability of the marsh to cleanse the drinking water and fuel the economies of fishing and tourism will be in doubt as well."

In the 1980s, a new study proved that the Everglades are vital in providing fresh water for the 3.5 million human residents of South Florida. Most of the rainfall that the region depends on for water comes from evaporation of the Everglades. "If you don't have rain and water, South Florida will become a desert—it's as simple as that," Douglas stated. Still, people continued to try to manipulate the Everglades in the name of progress—draining some areas to irrigate farmland or provide drinking water to cities, and flooding other areas when it appeared that rivers and canals in residential areas might overflow. Each artificial change in the water level affected the entire system, including the plants and animals. In 1983, the Everglades experienced a severe flood, causing the deaths of hundreds of deer and innumerable other animals from starvation or drowning. "A century after man first started to dominate the Everglades, that progress has stumbled. Consequences have started to catch up," Douglas noted. "It is, perhaps, an opportunity. The great wet wilderness of South Florida need not be degraded to a permanent state of mediocrity. If the people will it, if they enforce their will on the managers of Florida's future, the Everglades can be restored to nature's design."

In 1988, Douglas published her autobiography, *Marjory Stoneman Douglas: Voice of the River*. Praised by reviewers as "a delightful portrait of an indomitable lady" and "a lesson in courage," the book helped Douglas to become an inspiration to people all over the world. She has remained active in the fight to preserve the Everglades into the 1990s. "There are no other Everglades in the world," she explained. "They are, they have always been, one of the unique regions of the earth, remote, never wholly known." Though she is now nearly blind, she stated that "No matter how poor my eyes are I can still talk. I'll talk about the Everglades at the drop of a hat."

On the occasion of her 100th birthday, Florida Senator Bob Graham read the following tribute to Douglas before the U.S. Congress: "As we celebrate her 100th birthday, we remind ourselves of other lessons taught by Mrs. Douglas. That life should be lived to its fullest. That in every setback there is a silver lining. That we are the watchmen and women of all that surrounds us. It is ours to protect. And ours to preserve. We hope that each new generation will produce its own Marjory Stoneman Douglas, to devote his or her life to preserving our natural resources." In 1993, at the age of 103, Douglas received the Presidential Medal of Freedom—the nation's highest civilian honor. As he presented her with the award, President Bill Clinton said, "Mrs. Douglas, the next time I hear someone mention the timeless wonders and powers of Mother Nature, I'll be thinking about you."

MARRIAGE AND FAMILY

Marjory Stoneman married Kenneth Douglas, a newspaper editor 30 years her senior, in April 1914. The couple soon found that they had little in common, however, and they were divorced in April 1917. They did not have any children.

At the age of 106, Douglas continues to live in the simple, stucco cottage she built in Coconut Grove in the 1920s. She claims that her small home, nestled in the trees, "fits me like a glove." It contains many shelves to hold her large collection of books.

SELECTED WRITINGS

The Everglades: River of Grass, 1947 (revised edition, 1988)
Road to the Sun, 1951
Freedom River, 1953 (juvenile)
Hurricane, 1958
Alligator Crossing, 1959 (juvenile)
Florida: The Long Frontier, 1967
Marjory Stoneman Douglas: Voice of the River, 1988 (with John Rothchild)

HONORS AND AWARDS

O. Henry Memorial Short Story Collection: 1928, second prize
Conservationist of the Year (Florida Audubon Society): 1975
Conservationist of the Year (Florida Wildlife Federation): 1976
Alumnae Achievement Award (Wellesley College): 1977
Achievement Award (National Association for State and Local History and Florida Historical Association): 1978
Floridian of the Year Award (*Orlando Sentinel*): 1983
Presidential Medal of Freedom: 1993

FURTHER READING

BOOKS

Contemporary Authors, New Revision Series, Vol. 2
Douglas, Marjory Stoneman. *Marjory Stoneman Douglas: Voice of the River,* 1988 (with John Rothchild)
Keene, Ann T. *Earthkeepers: Observers and Protectors of Nature,* 1994
Sawyer, Kem Knapp. *Marjory Stoneman Douglas: Guardian of the Everglades,* 1994 (juvenile)

PERIODICALS

Current Biography 1953
Family Circle, Sep. 1, 1996, p.15
Knight-Ridder/Tribune News Service, Nov. 30, 1993, p.113; May 6, 1994, p.5
Ms., Jan.-Feb. 1989, p.68
Time, Dec. 13, 1993, p.31

ADDRESS

3774 Stewart Ave.
Coconut Grove, FL 33133

Dave Foreman 1946-
American Environmental Activist
Co-Founder of Earth First!
Chairman of the Wildlands Project

BIRTH

Dave Foreman was born on October 18, 1946, in Albuquerque, New Mexico, to Benjamin "Skip" Foreman, an Air Force pilot, and his wife, Lorane. Foreman was the oldest of three children; his brother, Steve, was born in 1953, and his sister, Roxanne, was born in 1955.

YOUTH

Since his father was in the military, Dave Foreman and his family rarely lived in one town for very long. By the time Dave was 13 years old, the Foremans had moved 11 times, relocating to such diverse places as New Mexico, Nevada, Texas, California, Bermuda, and the Philippines. "Wherever they moved, the Foremans remained part of the military establishment, with its rows of whitewashed houses and PX [military store] privileges," wrote Susan Zakin in *Coyotes and Town Dogs: Earth First! and the Environmental Movement.* "Only the scenery changed, from the tropics, where loneliness mingled with exoticism, to culturally barren American towns where the only aesthetic was the magnificent, sculptured desert sky."

Because his family moved so often, young Foreman found that as soon as he had made friends in one town, he was forced to leave for another one. All these moves, along with his small size—he was still under five feet tall when he was in tenth grade—made life tough for him. Lorane Foreman recalled that "he was so small and so smart, when he started school none of the kids would have anything to do with him because they thought he was a child prodigal or something."

But while the constant relocations from one community to another made it difficult for the shy Foreman to make friends, he found happiness in other areas. He loved animals with a passion, and spent hours studying books about all sorts of creatures, from spiders to falcons to mountain lions. "My favorite books, even before I could read, were two volumes from the American Museum of Natural History: *American Wildlife Illustrated* and *Wildlife the World Over Illustrated,*" wrote Foreman. "I remember my mother reading them to me when I was five years old; I still have them in my library. Unfortunately, my family was not one of bushwhackers; a picnic in the Sandia Mountains was about the closest we came to a wilderness experience. I could scarcely wait to turn 11 and join the Boy Scouts. I completed the requirements for Eagle Scout at the age of 13, and went on my first backpack trip, in Washington's Glacier Peak Wilderness Area, in 1962 with my Scout troop. That trip made me a wilderness fanatic."

As a teenager, Foreman also became very interested in religion, in part because of his admiration for Reverend Asa Lipscomb, a family friend. For a while he even thought about becoming a minister himself, but that ambition faded over the course of the next several years.

EDUCATION

Foreman attended many schools during his childhood and teenage years. He was scarcely noticed at some of these schools, since he was so small and he was rarely around for more than a year or two. By 11th grade, though, Foreman's stalled growth finally resumed, and he sprouted up to a relatively normal height of five feet, six inches tall. He became more confident in himself as a result, and he was even named class president at the high school in Blaine, Washington, that he was attending that year. Before Dave's senior year, though, Skip Foreman's military assignments made it necessary for the family to move once again, this time to Blythe, a small California community located in the center of the Mojave Desert. "I think that move hurt David more than any of the others he ever had," said his mother, "because he was really starting to have some fun."

After graduating from the high school in Blythe, Foreman spent a year attending a junior college in Texas. He then transferred to the University of New Mexico for the 1965 fall semester. By the time he had started college, Foreman's interest in politics had grown rapidly—he had even been a high school volunteer for Republican Barry Goldwater's 1964 presidential campaign. At the University of New Mexico, he was interested in all sorts of subjects, and he changed his major on a number of occasions as new passions surfaced.

Foreman stayed involved in politics, and in 1966 he became state chairman of Young Americans for Freedom, a conservative youth organization. He also emerged as a big supporter of American involvement in Vietnam during this time, in part because he had been "brought up on tales of a global communist conspiracy," as Zakin noted.

In 1967 Foreman decided to enlist in the military and go fight against the Communists in the Vietnam War. By this time he had grown into a tall and beefy young man, and he knew that many men his age were being drafted into the service anyway. He subsequently enlisted in the Marine Corps. The idea, Zakin wrote, "was to be a war hero, go to law school, then run for Congress."

MILITARY SERVICE

Once he was in the military, though, Foreman struggled badly. Other recruits at the Marine base in Quantico, Virginia, ridiculed him for his poor coordination, and within a short period of time he found himself on the receiving end of a constant barrage of verbal and physical abuse from other soldiers. Desperate to get out of the military, he sent a letter to his commander in which he proclaimed that he was a Communist. The Marines promptly transferred him to an area that housed other "problem" recruits, and Foreman waited to find out what would happen to him.

When Foreman learned that he was about to be transferred to the Marine installation at Parris Island for training as a regular enlisted man, he panicked. He had heard that Parris Island was known as an even more violent and brutal place than Quantico. Foreman ran away and hid in the Sandia Mountains of New Mexico before friends finally talked him into giving himself up.

Foreman spent a month in the Marine Corps brig before being released from military service with an undesirable discharge. He moved in with his parents, but the tension between him and his father, a career military man, sometimes seemed unbearable. At one point, Skip Foreman even told his son that he wished he had been killed in Vietnam rather than dishonor his family so badly. Dave Foreman and his father eventually reconciled, but it took years of struggle for them to repair their relationship. Looking back on this period, Foreman remarked that "I was crazy as a bedbug through-out this period and for a year afterwards."

CAREER HIGHLIGHTS

In the early 1970s Foreman retreated to the wilderness that he had always loved in order to recover from these experiences. He supported himself with a variety of odd jobs, including shoeing horses, teaching on a Zuni Indian reservation, and serving as a night clerk at a lonely trading post. He spent much of his free time backpacking and rafting down rivers, trying to figure out what he was going to do with the rest of his life.

In late 1971 Foreman was introduced to a number of people associated with the Black Mesa Defense Fund, an energetic environmental group that was trying to save a beautiful area of desert highland from proposed coal mining. Despite three years of hard work to stop the mining, the group's efforts failed. But Foreman's involvement in the battle triggered his life-long commitment to conservation causes.

THE WILDERNESS SOCIETY

Foreman immersed himself in a number of environmental causes around the American Southwest, and he quickly displayed a talent for waging tough, confrontational campaigns. Impressed with his charisma and energy, the Wilderness Society—one of the country's largest environmental organizations—asked him to join them as their principal consultant in New Mexico.

From 1973 to 1980, Foreman rose to become one of the Wilderness Society's most visible figures. He launched several effective campaigns against polluters and people who wanted to develop wilderness areas throughout the Southwest, and he soon was regarded as one of the organization's most passionate and powerful public speakers. During this same period Foreman established close friendships with several other conservationists; this crew of rowdy, hard-partying activists became known in environmental circles as the Buckaroos. Foreman and his fellow Buckaroos occasionally took great delight in ruffling the feathers of other environmentalists, who sometimes seemed more comfortable in legislative committees than the canyons and forests of the wilderness, and they enjoyed their wild reputation. But the Buckaroos never lost sight of their primary goal: protecting the environment.

By the late 1970s, though, Foreman felt frustrated with all the compromises that the conservation community was making with government officials and business interests. He became particularly angry after learning in 1979 that millions of acres of forest were going to be opened to development under a Forest Service plan known as RARE (Roadless Area Review and Evaluation) II. "We [the environmental community] had lost to the timber, mining, and cattle interests on every point," Foreman wrote. "What had backfired? I thought again about the different approaches to RARE II: the moderate, subdued one advanced by the major conservation groups; the howling, impassioned, extreme stand set forth by off-road-vehicle zealots, many ranchers, local boosters, loggers, and miners. They looked like fools. We looked like statesman. They won."

Fed up with what he saw as ineffective efforts to protect the environment among the leading conservation organizations—and concerned about leadership changes in the Wilderness Society—Foreman resigned from his position in June 1980.

BIRTH OF EARTH FIRST!

In the spring of 1980, Foreman and four other conservationists—Mike Roselle, Bart Koehler, Howie Wolke, and Ron Kezar—went on a camping trip deep into the heart of the Pinacate Desert, a national park in northern Mexico. During the journey the five men talked about their love of the wilderness and complained that it felt as if they were fighting a losing battle. They talked about the need for a more radical environmental group, such as the one that turned to sabotage and civil disobedience in Edward Abbey's novel *The Monkey Wrench Gang* (see entry on Edward Abbey in this volume of *Biography Today*). They all agreed that the environment needed a defender that would be as confrontational and belligerent as the forces that threatened it. Before they knew it, Foreman and the others had decided that they could launch such a group themselves. They called this new group Earth First! Ron Kezar later told Zakin that "if Earth First! hadn't come along, somebody else would have come along with something like it. It was an idea whose time had come."

Earth First! developed quickly over the next several months, but as its founders intended, it was quite different from other environmental organizations. Rik Scarce remarked in *Eco-Warriors* that "Earth First! was to be like a Plains Indian tribe, existing in autonomous groups which shared the same beliefs. There would be no bureaucracy, no lobbyists, no organizational spokespeople, just a force of devoted, unpaid, grassroots activists occupying a niche they had created for themselves in the environmental movement. . . . Perhaps most telling, there was to be no membership. The closest things to membership cards are T-shirts with Roselle's clenched-fist logo and the motto, 'No Compromise in Defense of Mother Earth.'"

On July 4, 1980, only a few days after Foreman submitted his resignation to the Wilderness Society, Earth First! held a "Round River Rendezvous" that attracted more than 200 people. A few months later, Foreman and Koehler started a trip around the country to drum up support for the group and its views. As the weeks passed, small Earth First! chapters sprang up around the country.

Earth First! came to national attention in 1981, when it unfurled a 300-foot-long plastic streamer down the face of Glen Canyon Dam on the Colorado River in southern Utah. The streamer, which looked like a large, black crack in the dam's surface, was meant to convey the group's anger at the loss of Glen Canyon, a region of legendary beauty that had been flooded when the dam became operational back in the 1960s. The crowd that watched the event included a number of reporters as well as Edward Abbey, whose nature writings were a continuing source of inspiration for the members of Earth First!

The action at Glen Canyon Dam was widely reported, both in environmental publications and in the usual media outlets. Earth First! had made an immediate impact. "The crack symbolized a break with environmentalism's past," wrote Rik Scarce. "No more muddling through. No more compromise. Earth First! would be there to at least try to stop that which the mainstream had given up on or never paid attention to. After the crack the environmental movement would never again be the same."

Over the next several years, the unusual personalities and methods of Earth First! kept them in the news. In addition to conducting protests and other actions practiced by other environmental groups, members of the Earth First! organization advocated all sorts of illegal activities, from tree spiking—in which steel spikes are driven into trees to destroy logging equipment—to pulling up surveying stakes. They also targeted billboards, which they saw as an ugly blot on the wild, and heavy mining and construction equipment used in tearing up wilderness lands. Such activities, which came to be known as "monkeywrenching," were heavily criticized by many business interests—and even some environmentalists. Defenders of monkeywrenching pointed out that civil disobedience had been used in the past by Americans to protest such practices as slavery.

But some critics charged that the group's monkeywrenching activities amounted to nothing more than dangerous vandalism, and animosity between Earth First! and some loggers, miners, and developers soon rose to ominous levels.

Foreman, meanwhile, became firmly entrenched as Earth First!'s leading voice. He traveled all around the nation during the 1980s, delivering rousing speeches intended to attract more people to environmental activism. "We've got to encounter the problem, we've got to encounter the magnitude, the enormity of what our generation is doing to the planet," he told his audiences. "I'm flesh and blood. The winds fill my lungs, the mountains make my bones, the oceans run through my veins. I'm an animal and I'll never be anything but an animal. When a chain saw rips into a 2,000-

year-old redwood tree, it's ripping into my guts. When a bulldozer plows through a virgin hillside, it's plowing through my side, and when a bullet knocks down a grizzly bear or a wolf, it's going through my heart."

PROBLEMS IN EARTH FIRST!

By 1986, however, problems within Earth First! hampered the group's conservation efforts. Foreman recognized that a growing number of people in the group were a bit strange, and he worried that some of the people who had joined the cause were less interested in protecting the environment than in other causes. He even began to suspect that some of them were simply using the group's rowdy reputation as an excuse for drunken, obnoxious behavior.

In addition, the lack of organization within Earth First! was making it hard for the group to address concerns effectively. The founders of the organization had wanted to give each local group the freedom to do whatever they wanted without getting bogged down in bureaucratic red tape, but it was proving difficult to coordinate activities. Foreman found that when one group did something stupid, it reflected badly on all of Earth First! Late in 1989, for instance, Foreman and other members of Earth First! were horrified to learn that one of the group's members had publicly burned the American flag. Sierra Club activist Doug Scott knew that the incident was a serious blow to Foreman and the other people who were dedicated to the principles of Earth First! "A movement's got to be brain dead to let the American flag get away from it as a symbol."

The organization was also engaged in an internal struggle over the appropriateness of some of its monkeywrenching activities, especially tree spiking. When a California logger was seriously injured in May 1987 while cutting through a spiked tree, industry spokesmen, government officials, and the national media all rebuked Earth First! for its role in the affair.

Earth First! leaders were confused by the whole incident, though. Conservationists were far more often the victims than the perpetrators of violence, yet the media had devoted little coverage to such incidents (Foreman himself had once been dragged under a construction truck for more than 100 yards by an angry driver). Moreover, the spike that injured the logger had been in a relatively young tree that had already been cut down; Earth First! typically targeted loggers who were going after healthy ancient forests. In addition, Earth First! policy was to always make sure that a warning phone call was made to area lumber mills after a spiking took place so that loggers would not be injured. Foreman and others pointed out that with this policy in place, no loggers had ever been hurt by an Earth First! tree spiking excursion. The authorities later determined that the prime suspect in the incident was actually a right-wing neighbor in the area who was prone to strange military fantasies, but the damage was done. Some environmental groups even contended that the controversy swirling around Earth First! was hurting the effort to protect wilderness. Foreman began to wonder if the group's critics might be right.

Foreman continued to work to protect various wilderness areas around the country for the next several years, but he withdrew somewhat from Earth First!'s daily activities. In 1989 he handed over ownership of the *Earth First! Journal*, the group's magazine, to a nonprofit organization established by the journal's staff. Around that same period he made remarks on the subjects of famine, AIDS, and immigration that outraged many people. Like many environmentalists, Foreman viewed overpopulation as a major factor contributing to the destruction of the environment. But he took this position to an extreme, suggesting that AIDS had the positive effect of reducing human population. Those who thought that he sounded bigoted and cold-hearted included some of his friends and allies. Tired and bitter about the changes taking place in Earth First!, Foreman began to ponder leaving the group.

ARRESTED BY FBI

In May 1989 Foreman was dragged out of bed at gunpoint by FBI agents. He and a few other activists were charged with destroying ski resort property and being part of a conspiracy to damage power lines leading to three nuclear power plants in Arizona, California, and Colorado. Some months before, assisted by informers and undercover agents, the FBI had learned that a few members of Earth First! were planning to damage power lines and other aspects of the plants' operations. They were determined to arrest Foreman, too, even though he was not involved in the plot. The FBI apparently felt that if they nabbed a well-known person such as Foreman, it would teach the other Earth First! activists a lesson. After a long period of surveillance they finally got evidence that, while Foreman was not taking a direct part in the action, he at least had a hazy understanding that something was going to take place.

A high-powered attorney agreed to take Foreman's case for free, so he spent only a few days in jail before he was released on bond. After several delays, Foreman's case finally came before a judge in 1991. At this time, Foreman agreed to plead guilty to a reduced felony conspiracy charge. As part of the agreement his sentencing was delayed for five years, after which the charge would be reduced to a misdemeanor. The other four people who were arrested on conspiracy charges received sentences ranging from one month to six years in jail. Their heavier sentences caused some hard feelings towards Foreman within the Earth First! movement as well.

THE WILDLANDS PROJECT

With the trial behind him, Foreman quietly resumed his life. His involvement with Earth First! had come to a close in 1990 — "it is time for me to build a campfire elsewhere" was how he put it — but he remained very interested in environmental activism. He worked on a couple of books on conservation issues, and in 1993 he launched a new campaign called the Wildlands Project. The Wildlands Project hopes to establish an interconnected series of large wilderness preserves across America. "Conservation biologists tell us we must go beyond our current national park, wildlife refuge, and wilderness area systems," he wrote in *Sierra*. "What's needed are large wilderness cores, buffer zones, and biological corridors. The cores would be managed to protect and, where necessary, restore native biological diversity and natural processes."

In 1995 Foreman was elected to the board of directors of the Sierra Club, but he continued to spend a great deal of his time and energy on the Wildlands Project. "I'm trying to articulate a vision of restoring wilderness across North America," he told *Outside*. "Quite frankly, what I'm doing now is more the real 'me' than my reputation with Earth First!, but I'm not apologizing in the least for Earth First!"

Foreman believes that such plans as the Wildlands Project will prove to be useful tools in conservationist efforts to defend America's natural resources. "It is no small benefit that a vision of wilderness recovery allows us to show what conservationists are *for*. Too often, activists are dismissed as negative, whining doomsayers. By developing long-term proposals for wilderness, we say: 'Here is our vision for what North America should look like.' Civilization and wilderness can coexist. By acting responsibly with respect for the land, we can become a better people,'" he wrote in 1995. Management plans like the Wildlands Project, he added, "wrest the fundamental debate from those who would gladly plunder our natural heritage. Do we have the generosity of spirit, the greatness of heart to share the land with other species? I think we do."

In the mid-1990s, even after more than 20 years of controversy and pitched battles, Foreman remained dedicated to encouraging people to defend the country's rivers, forests, and creatures. "My way is not the only good way," he admitted. "My style is not the only valid style. Thus I do not want to tell anyone what to do. Each of us has to find his or her own role, style, and tools to use in defense of Earth. These may change through time and situation. Wearing a suit and tie, I have sat in a room alone with a United States senator, going over boundary lines on a map of a Wilderness proposal. I've also worn camouflage, prowling around a forest, pulling up survey stakes for a road. What is important is that you do something. Now."

MARRIAGE AND FAMILY

Foreman's first marriage, to Debbie Sease, lasted from 1975 to 1979. He later married Nancy Morton, a nurse and environmental activist whom he met during his Earth First! days. He has no children, which he has said is in keeping with his long-standing warnings about the negative effects of overpopulation on the planet.

WRITINGS

Ecodefense: A Field Guide to Monkeywrenching, 1985
Defending the Earth, 1990 (with Murray Bookchin)
Confessions of an Eco-Warrior, 1991
The Big Outside, 1992 (with Howie Wolke)

FURTHER READING

BOOKS

Davis, John. *Earth First! Reader: Ten Years of Radical Environmentalism*, 1991
Foreman, Dave. *Confessions of an Eco-Warrior*, 1991
Scarce, Rik. *Eco-Warriors*, 1990
Zakin, Susan. *Coyotes and Town Dogs: Earth First! and the Environmental Movement*, 1993

PERIODICALS

Buzzworm, Mar./Apr. 1990, p.48
Esquire, Feb. 1987, p.99
GARBAGE, Spring 1994, p.32
Knight-Ridder/Tribune News Service, Dec. 10, 1993, p.121
Mother Jones, Nov./Dec. 1990, p.77; Nov./Dec. 1991, p.20
Outside, Nov. 1995, p.74; Oct. 1996, p.46
People Weekly, Apr. 16, 1990, p.113
The Progressive, Sep. 1989, p.15
Sierra, Sept./Oct. 1995, p.52
Sports Illustrated, May 27, 1991, p.54
U.S. News & World Report, Sep. 17, 1990, p.50

ADDRESS

The Wildlands Project
1955 West Grant Road
Suite 148 A
Tucson, AZ 85745

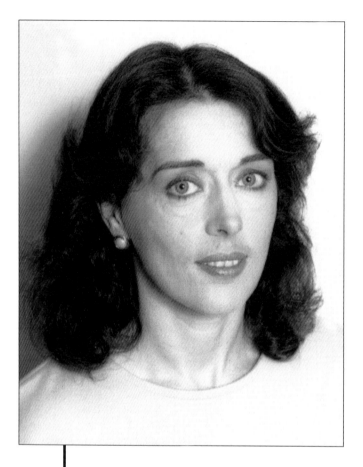

Lois Gibbs   1951-
American Homemaker Turned
Environmental Activist
Organized Residents of Love Canal
Community against Toxic Waste Threat
Founder and Director of Citizens
Clearinghouse for Hazardous Wastes

BIRTH AND EARLY LIFE

Lois Marie Gibbs has released very little information to the
public about her childhood. It is known, however, that she
was born on June 25, 1951, to Patricia Ann Conn. As she grew
up she was known as a shy child. On one occasion she even

skipped school because of her nervousness over presenting a book report in front of her classmates. In 1969 she graduated from Grand Island High School in Grand Island, a suburb of Buffalo, New York.

MARRIAGE AND FAMILY

A short time after graduating from high school, Lois married Harry Gibbs, and they started a family. They had a son, Michael, in 1972, and a daughter, Melissa (Missy), in 1975. Neither Gibbs nor her husband had gone on to college, but they managed to put together a nice middle-class existence for themselves and their children. Around the time that Michael was born, the couple bought a modest house in Niagara Falls, New York. The house was not that big, and they needed to do some work on it—Lois and Harry refinished the basement themselves—but Harry's steady employment as a chemical worker allowed Lois to stay at home and care for their children after they were born.

In addition, the couple really liked the area, which was marked by small but neatly kept yards and homes. "It was a lovely neighborhood in a quiet residential area, with lots of trees and lots of children outside playing," Gibbs recalled. Everything that they needed seemed conveniently located, too. The school that their children would attend was even within walking distance of their home. Sadly, though, the families in the area were unaware that the ground beneath that soil had been contaminated with nearly 22,000 tons of deadly chemicals over the course of more than 30 years.

HISTORY OF LOVE CANAL

In the first years of the 20th century, a businessman named William T. Love had proposed connecting upper and lower sections of the Niagara River by means of a several-mile-long canal.

The project was halted, though, when financial support for it dwindled. The partially dug "Love Canal" was abandoned until 1920, when the trench was made a municipal and chemical disposal site. For more than 30 years the canal was filled with garbage from the city of Niagara Falls, chemicals from the Hooker Chemical Corporation, and waste—including possible chemical warfare materials—from the U.S. Army.

In 1953 Hooker Chemical Corporation filled in the trench and covered it with dirt. They then sold the 16-acre parcel of land to the Board of Education for $1. The sale agreement, though, included a stipulation that said that Hooker would not be responsible for any illnesses or deaths that might occur in the future because of the buried hazardous waste.

The Niagara Falls School Board knew that thousands of tons of hazardous chemicals had been buried at Love Canal, but it decided to put the land to use anyway. Within three years of the sale, an elementary school and a growing number of houses sat on the buried canal area. By the late 1950s, some residents of the neighborhood had begun to complain about nauseating odors and hot, sludgy sections of ground, but their concerns were ignored.

Throughout the 1960s and most of the 1970s, some families in the area asked local, state, and federal agencies to check on their concerns, but nobody paid much attention. Most of the people who complained thought that they were alone in their concerns; they were unaware that other families were worried as well. Meanwhile, the few people who knew about the dangerous chemicals buried at Love Canal kept their mouths shut. The secret was kept until June 1978, when Lois Gibbs, a quiet young homemaker with no college education and little interest in politics or current events, began to suspect that something scary was lurking in her family's neighborhood.

CAREER HIGHLIGHTS

99TH STREET SCHOOL

In June 1978 Gibbs grew increasingly concerned about the tone of a number of articles that were published in the *Niagara Falls Gazette.* The newspaper reported that some neighborhood residents were concerned about the unhealthy state of trees and shrubs in the area, while others were upset about the industrial odors that always seemed present. The articles, which suggested that some of the chemicals that had been buried in the Love Canal area might be dangerous, aroused her curiosity. Still, "I paid little attention" at first, she admitted. "I thought it was terrible; but I lived on the other side of Pine Avenue. Those poor people over there on the other side were the ones who had to worry. The problem didn't affect me, so I wasn't going to bother doing anything about it . . . Then when I found out the 99th Street School was indeed on top of it, I was alarmed. My son attended that school. He was in kindergarten that year. I decided I needed to do some investigating."

Looking over back issues of the local newspaper, Gibbs was stunned at the number of articles that had been published over the years on Love Canal. Concerned that her son, who had developed epilepsy only a few months after starting school, was being hurt by the chemicals buried beneath the school, Gibbs called the superintendent of schools. She told him that she wanted to move her son to another of the public schools in Niagara Falls, but the official refused to allow it. He argued that if they transferred Michael because the school area was contaminated, then they would have to move all the children. "The superintendent said that he did not believe the area was contaminated, and, finally, that they weren't about to close the 99th Street School," Gibbs recalled. "I was disappointed and angry. School would open again in two months, and I wasn't going to let my child go back to that school. I didn't care what I had to do to prevent it. I wasn't going to send him to a private school, either. First of all, we couldn't afford it; and second, I thought parents had the right to send their children to schools that were safe."

GROWING HEALTH CONCERNS

Gibbs decided to start a petition drive in the neighborhood. As she went from door-to-door, she heard a frightening number of stories that added to her growing fears. "It seemed as though every home on 99th street had someone with an illness," she said. "The more I heard, the more frightened I became. . . . The entire community seemed to be sick!" Gibbs was particularly shocked by the large number of birth defects and crib deaths that families in the Love Canal area had endured. As the number of signatures on her petition grew, she became increasingly convinced that something was terribly wrong in her neighborhood.

Later that month, the New York State Health Department held a meeting in the community to discuss the complaints that people had made. Several community members told department officials stories about children who had burned their feet and dogs who had burned their noses merely by touching the ground. Gibbs was even more alarmed when she heard this, for it was an indication that chemicals were seeping to the surface in some areas. The officials told their audience that they were investigating, but other than warning people not to eat food out of their gardens, they had little to say. "People began walking out, muttering, furious," Gibbs said. "There were no answers. They didn't understand, and they were becoming frightened."

By this time, people in the neighborhood were eager to talk to Gibbs, who was emerging as a community leader. One woman told Gibbs that the health department had paid her 11-year-old child to retrieve "hot" rocks from the Love Canal area. "It amazed me that the health department would do such a thing. They are supposed to protect people's health, and here they were jeopardizing an innocent child. I used to have a lot of faith in officials, especially doctors and experts. Now I was losing that faith—fast!"

In August 1978 Gibbs and fellow activist Debbie Cerrillo met with a number of health department officials and doctors involved in the Love Canal investigation. "The bombshell came when [Health Department Commissioner Whalen] recommended the evacuation of pregnant women and children under age two," she said. The state said that it would not provide any sort of assistance to those people; it simply recommended that they get out, leaving their families behind. "With that I almost lost my cool," Gibbs wrote. "I was furious. I jumped up and said to Commissioner Whalen: 'If the dump will hurt pregnant women and children under two, what, for God's sake, is it going to do to the rest of us!? What do you think you're doing?'" Gibbs noted that Cerrillo, who was scared and angry, also registered her disbelief. "Between the two of us, we kept the meeting in an uproar for some 15 minutes. 'We can't eat out of our garden. We can't go in our backyard. We can't have children under two. We can't be pregnant. You're telling us it's safe for the rest of us!'"

When Gibbs and Cerrillo returned home, they met with their neighbors, who had been hoping for reassurance that their homes and families were safe. Instead, Gibbs had to tell them that the officials had offered practically no other information except for their warning about infants and pregnant women. "I tried to sympathize with them and explain what I had learned," wrote Gibbs. "In hindsight, it's almost impossible to describe that evening. It was horrible to see all those people so afraid, helpless, and angry, not knowing what to do or where to turn."

LOVE CANAL HOMEOWNERS ASSOCIATION

On August 4, 1978, Gibbs and other community leaders formed the Love Canal Homeowners Association, a group that they hoped would give them a unified voice. A week later, New York Governor Hugh Carey announced that the state would purchase a small group of homes that were right next to Love Canal and relocate the families. He also said that state agencies would continue their investigation into the area. Many of these families were relieved at the news, although some were bitter because their children had already been struck with birth defects and other illnesses. The other residents of the neighborhood, meanwhile, could do little but go back to their homes and wait for the government's test results.

As the weeks went by, Gibbs watched the health department workers as they gathered data. Their efforts seemed both disorganized and careless to her, and she and others repeatedly warned them that they needed to be more careful with the materials they were handling, but their warnings were ignored. State officials continued to hold meetings with the residents of Love Canal during this time, but Gibbs and her neighbors came away from these sessions even more frustrated and confused. The doctors and administrators they talked with provided little information about their findings, and the information they did offer often contradicted what they had said earlier.

The Love Canal Homeowners Association launched their own investigation with the help of a few sympathetic health experts, and they were shocked at what they found. Their scientific research confirmed that

cancers, birth defects, miscarriages, epilepsy cases, urinary disorders, and other health problems were extremely high in Love Canal and surrounding neighborhoods, and that deadly poisons such as dioxin — which can cause liver disease, nervous disorders, birth defects, stillbirths, and cancer — were present in their air, water, and soil in very high concentrations. Many families sent petitions to the state government pleading with it to relocate them. These families had nearly all their money invested in their homes; they did not have the money to leave without the state's help.

Throughout the fall of 1978, Love Canal families waited to hear whether the government would deliver them from their nightmare, or even whether the department of health and other agencies would start leveling with them. Instead, municipal, state, and federal officials continued to insist that Gibbs and her allies were overreacting. "I would laugh if it weren't so tragic," wrote Gibbs. "The school board and the city knew what was in the canal and what kind of poisons were going into the Niagara River; but they blamed us for ruining Niagara Falls with bad publicity!"

TRAGEDIES IN LOVE CANAL

In the meantime, people in the neighborhood continued to fall ill. Gibbs reflected that "I had never seen so many men crying." On one occasion a man who lived a few streets over from Gibbs came into her association office and began crying. "His neighbor's seven-year-old boy had just died. [He] believed the child's death was related to Love Canal," she recalled. "This little boy had been playing baseball and football. He showed no sign of illness. All of a sudden, his body swelled up. He was hospitalized twice, and then he died. He had apparently been a healthy, normal child. The man, who had been close to the boy, sat there and cried his eyes out." By this time Gibbs had heard many such terrible stories, and all she could do was sit there and think: "Oh God, isn't this ever going to end? Everyone who comes in here is crying about something that breaks your heart just to hear it."

One fall day in 1978, all the families of Love Canal who had asked to be relocated learned that their requests had been denied by the state. "People didn't know what to do or where to go from here," said Gibbs. "There was no appeal. The tension was powerful—people crying, throwing their hands up, pacing back and forth, walking up and down staircases, just not knowing what to do. . . . More than anything else, this incident convinced me we would have to fight for our interests—and our lives. The state had lied to us. We believed them when they said they would help us." Instead, Gibbs said, the state had turned its back. "Some of the residents couldn't handle the disappointment; one or two were talking about suicide, and not idly, either. They were deadly serious. And New York State had no feelings for them. The state didn't want to spend the money, and that's all there was to it."

The state's rejection of the relocation petitions had been a tremendous blow to everyone's spirits, but Gibbs and the other members of the Love Canal Homeowners Association picked themselves up and continued the fight. Reporters and other media people sought Gibbs out for interviews, and she even made an appearance on the "Phil Donahue Show." The association also staged pickets and protests, and during one of them Gibbs was arrested and thrown in jail. "My arrest bothered my son," Gibbs wrote. "He wanted to know if I was a bad guy. Why did I do that? Only bad people got arrested. He was only six then, and couldn't understand."

In February 1979 the New York State Health Department announced that pregnant women and families with children under the age of two in Love Canal would be relocated, with the state picking up the tab for their moving and relocation expenses and their rent (the residents were still responsible for the mortgage payments on their homes). The families of Love Canal were furious when they heard the news. "You can't play games with my life," one crying woman told Health Commissioner Axelrod. "If it is going to hurt pregnant women and children under two, it's going to hurt me."

Gibbs later admitted that she thought about getting pregnant just so she could escape from Love Canal for two years. But she then discovered that the last two children born on her street had had birth defects. "I didn't want to take a chance on having a malformed child just because we had to get out of Love Canal," she said. "I couldn't afford to stay, and I couldn't afford to leave. I didn't know whether all of the fighting with the state was going to help. It took us so long to get so few concessions."

THE KILLING GROUND

A few months later, in the spring of 1979, ABC broadcast a documentary about the Love Canal situation called "The Killing Ground" that brought national attention to the situation. Officials of Niagara Falls, including the mayor, the city manager, and business leaders, were furious with the show. They accused Gibbs of betraying the city, and one convention center official confronted her, saying, "I will never get anyone in there now, with this on national news. Who's going to come to Niagara Falls for a convention?" Unfazed, Gibbs replied, "Your convention center is worth what our houses are worth—right now, zero. Now you know how it feels to be a victim of Love Canal."

Throughout 1979 Gibbs and the Love Canal Homeowners Association petitioned the state government to be relocated. The state finally agreed to let some families move into motels at state expense for a temporary period. Such small victories gave the group the courage to keep fighting. When Gibbs and her allies learned that New York State had turned down financial and scientific assistance from federal agencies who had heard about Love Canal, the association publicized the action, embarrassing the state government. Gibbs later explained that the state agencies turned down the help because they did not want anyone to know what a poor job they had done. "[They] did their studies so poorly that none of them would stand up in court," she charged. "None of them would stand up to scientific criticism."

By late 1979 about 150 families from Love Canal (including Gibbs and her family) were living in motels and Niagara University dorms at state expense. "The motel bill was $7,500 a day," said Gibbs, "and the state was threatening to throw families out and force them to return home. From one day till the next, the residents did not know where they would be the next morning. Their lives were disrupted, and so were the lives of their children."

The uncertainty seemed to come to an end, though, when the New York State Legislature passed a bill to permanently relocate Love Canal families in the fall of 1979. "We were all very, very happy," wrote Gibbs. "We celebrated, but it was to prove premature." When arrangements for their motel stays ended, the families still had not been told when they would be able to move. "After the governor's announcement [of the relocation], we debated whether we would try to stay in the motels until we were actually relocated. But people believed the governor would follow through; and besides they were tired," Gibbs recalled. "It was an eerie feeling when I walked into our house. I felt as if I didn't belong there. It was cold, dangerous, and very frightening. It wasn't my house anymore."

BACK IN LOVE CANAL

Gibbs and the other people of Love Canal waited impatiently for the re-location to begin. Instead, the days dragged by as the state tried to decide how many blocks of residents should be moved. In the meantime, residents were presented with constant reminders of the deadly poisons lurking beneath their feet. They learned that over the course of the previous year, only two out of 14 neighborhood pregnancies had resulted in normal births. "The rest," wrote Gibbs, "were stillborns or miscarriages. One poor child was born with his diaphragm and intestines outside his body. He had six operations and died in September 1980. Some had such birth defects as clubfoot and six toes. The fetus is a sensitive indicator. What was happening to babies that were being conceived and carried at Love Canal showed the potential and actual damage to our children and to us."

In May 1980 tensions in the neighborhood finally exploded. On May 17, representatives of the Environmental Protection Agency (EPA) arrived in the neighborhood to tell Love Canal residents about the results of chromosome tests the agency had performed on several dozen residents a few months before (chromosomes are cells that contain the DNA or RNA that comprise the genes of an individual). Even before the residents and their families arrived at the offices of the association to hear the news, though, they knew that the results were terribly depressing. Somebody at the EPA had already told the press that an alarming percentage of the people who had been tested (one out of three) had broken chromosomes; this meant that they carried a greater likelihood of falling victim to cancer, genetic damage, or other illnesses. At the same time, people in the neighborhood learned that the promised relocation of Love Canal families to safe places was in jeopardy. As the EPA officials met with each person individually, cries of sadness or relief rang down the office's hallways. "I tried to keep things running smoothly as best I could," Gibbs remembered, "but it was difficult to keep from being deeply moved by my friends' tears and their shock. I kept wondering how much more those people could take!"

Two days later, on May 19, two EPA officials were taken hostage in the Love Canal Homeowners Association offices by the angry, grief-stricken residents of Love Canal. They were held captive for only a few hours before Gibbs convinced the crowd to let them go, but even she knew that a tragedy had been narrowly averted. If the desperate pleas of the people of Love Canal continued to be ignored, there was no telling what might happen next.

VICTORY

The next day the EPA announced that the families of Love Canal would be relocated immediately, with the costs of the relocation picked up by the Federal Disaster Assistance Administration (FDAA). Gibbs and her neighbors were ecstatic. The nightmare was finally over. "Someone brought a case of champagne," Gibbs remembered. "Corks were popping. We were so happy. People were laughing, crying, hugging each other, dancing around, and saying: 'We won! We won! We're out!'"

In the fall of 1980 President Jimmy Carter signed an agreement with the state of New York appropriating $15 million to purchase 237 homes in Love Canal. Critics of the agreement complained that the area to be relocated was arrived at in a completely arbitrary fashion. Reporter Andrew Danzo noted in the *Washington Monthly* that "because the evacuation zone's northern boundary . . . runs down the middle of [a] creek, homeowners on the north bank were excluded from the government buyout, even though their side of the creek is just as contaminated as the side that is officially part of Love Canal." But the government refused to change the boundary.

By February 1981 more than 400 families had left the area, never to return. But even with the long struggle behind them, Gibbs points out that the memory of Love Canal will always be with those families. "Many have come to hate government, because they have been hurt so badly, lied to so often, and treated so horribly," she wrote in 1982. "Parents sometimes panic when their child has a common cold. There's always a concern whether it is a cold or the beginning of something worse because their children were exposed to toxic chemicals."

Indeed, Gibbs notes that even the children who remained physically healthy were traumatized by the whole experience. Torn from the homes they knew so well, separated from their favorite toys because of concerns about contamination, many small children suffered emotionally. "The total psychological damage to our children has not been measured, but it will stay with them for a long time," she said.

One thing that encouraged Gibb, though, was that both Occidental Petroleum, Hooker Chemical's parent company, and the city of Niagara Falls were eventually forced to pay for their irresponsible actions. The chemical company was forced to pay a $20 million fine for its dumping practices, and the city of Niagara was directed to provide financial compensation to Love Canal residents as well.

During the 1980s, the Environmental Protection Agency began the long and difficult task of cleaning up Love Canal. After a while the agency gave up trying to identify all of the estimated 200 different toxic chemicals that had been dumped there, and they concentrated their efforts on making the area habitable again. In 1990, after several years of clean-up activities, the Environmental Protection Agency announced that the Love Canal area was again safe. Despite its reputation, families rushed into the neighborhood, attracted by bargain prices for homes.

CITIZENS CLEARINGHOUSE FOR HAZARDOUS WASTES

After the Love Canal battle was concluded, Gibbs decided to continue her crusade against toxic chemicals and irresponsible corporate polluters. She formed an organization called the Citizens Clearinghouse for Hazardous Wastes (CCHW) to help communities across the nation organize against toxic threats. According to the CCHW, the organization "was established as a grassroots organization teaching people how to organize their communities, stand up for themselves and successfully challenge toxic dumpers."

Since 1980 the CCHW, which is located in Falls Church, Virginia, has worked with over 8,000 local community groups concerned about hazardous waste practices in their neighborhoods. The group was an important force in convincing McDonald's to abandon their environmentally unfriendly polystyrene packaging in the 1980s, and it continues to serve as one of the country's foremost proponents of environmental justice.

Throughout the organization's existence, Gibbs has been its leader. A tireless organizer, the formerly shy homemaker has delivered hundreds of lectures over the years, and she has been interviewed about environmental issues dozens of times on radio and television. She has also testified before both houses of Congress about hazardous waste issues. She was even the subject of a 1982 movie on CBS called *Lois Gibbs: The Love Canal Story*, which starred Marsha Mason.

Despite the inevitable disappointments that she has endured over the years — and her continuing concerns about the presence of dioxin and other deadly chemicals in our air and water — Gibbs remains upbeat about the future of the country. "This is a democracy," she said. "We do have the power; the problem is that they beat us down so much that people feel powerless. I think the challenge for the grassroots movement is to remove that feeling that you can't fight city hall, that you can't fight the statehouse. We need to let people understand and realize the fact that they are the biggest players in the circle, that they hold that vote — and if they exercise that vote in a positive way then they can control everything."

HOME AND FAMILY

Lois Gibbs and her husband and four children make their home in northern Virginia.

WRITINGS

Love Canal: My Story, 1982 (as told to Murray Levine)
Dying from Dioxin, 1995

HONORS AND AWARDS

Outstanding Citizen Award (Buffalo, NY): 1980
Citizen of the Year (National Association of Social Workers): 1980
Health Advocate of the Year (National Women's Health Network): 1980
Public Citizenship Award (New York Public Interest Group): 1980
Environmental Citizen of the Year (Clean Water Action Project): 1981
Dedicated Service Award (National Convention of Grassroots Leaders): 1986
Leadership Award (American Orthopsychiatric Association): 1987
Goldman Environmental Prize (for North America): 1990
OUTSIDE Magazine's Honor Roll—Ten Who Made a Difference: 1991
Certificate of Merit (Students Against Violating the Environment): 1992
Princeton Community Peace Prize: 1994
Christophers Award: 1995

FURTHER READING

BOOKS

Gibbs, Lois. *Dying from Dioxin*, 1995
———. *Love Canal: My Story*, 1982 (as told to Murray Levine)
Levine, Adeline. *Love Canal: Science, Politics, and People*, 1982
Wallace, Aubrey. *Eco-Heroes: Twelve Tales of Environmental Victory*, 1993
Who's Who in America, 1996

PERIODICALS

Cleveland Plain Dealer, Apr. 16, 1996, p.E1
People, Feb. 22, 1982, p.42; March 7, 1994, p.168
New York Times, May 21, 1980, sec.2, p.1; May 26, 1980, sec.2, p.1; June 5, 1980, sec.2, p.3
Newsweek, July 30, 1990, p.25
Olympian (Seattle), Jan. 12, 1996, p.A1
Time, Mar. 7, 1988, p.59; Apr. 23, 1990, p.79; May 28, 1990, p.27
Utne Reader, July/Aug. 1994, p.78
Washington Monthly, Sep. 1988, p.11

ADDRESS

Citizens Clearinghouse for Hazardous Wastes
P.O. Box 6806
Falls Church, VA 22040

WORLD WIDE WEB SITE

http://www.cais.net/wolf/cchw/cchw.html

Wangari Maathai   1940-
Kenyan Environmentalist, Feminist, Human
Rights Activist, and Educator
Founder of the Green Belt Movement

BIRTH

Wangari Muta Maathai was born on April 1, 1940, in Nyeri, a
town in south-central Kenya about 100 miles from Nairobi.
Her parents were subsistence farmers. She was the oldest
daughter among their six children.

YOUTH

Maathai grew up in a rural farming community as a member

of the Kikuyu tribe—one of Kenya's more successful and educated ethnic groups. Though most Kenyan girls were expected to help out with the household chores and remain with their families until they got married, Maathai was lucky enough to receive an education. "My parents were progressive people, and they decided that I should have a chance to go to school," she explained. "If they hadn't done that, I would probably never have left the farm."

EDUCATION

Maathai was an excellent student at Loreto Limuru Girls High School. Her teachers were so impressed by her abilities that they arranged for her to receive a scholarship to attend college in the United States. In 1960, she began taking courses at Mount St. Scholastica College in Atchison, Kansas. After earning a bachelor of science degree in biology in 1964, she went on to graduate school at the University of Pittsburgh. When she received her master of science degree in anatomy the following year, she became the first woman in eastern and central Africa to earn an advanced degree.

Though Maathai enjoyed her time in the United States, she never planned to remain there after completing her education. Instead, she always felt that "I had to go back home . . . and make a contribution." She returned to Kenya in 1966 and found that the knowledge she had gained was in high demand. She took a job as a research assistant in the department of veterinary medicine at the University of Nairobi, and she also began work on her doctoral degree there. In 1971, Maathai became the first woman to earn a Ph.D. from the university. She went on to achieve a number of other firsts in the academic arena as she became the first woman lecturer, professor, and department head at the University of Nairobi over the next few years.

CAREER HIGHLIGHTS

In the early 1970s, after she had married a prominent businessman and settled into a comfortable lifestyle, Maathai still yearned to make a contribution to society. This feeling grew even stronger when her husband decided to run for the Kenyan Parliament. As she accompanied her husband on his election campaign stops, she had the opportunity to meet and talk with many poor people who lived in the cities. She became deeply concerned about the conditions they lived in and the problems they faced. "I had grown up in a poor rural area, but it was nothing like what I encountered in the slums of Nairobi," Maathai recalled. "These people were desperate. All they wanted was a promise from my husband that we would find them jobs. Of course he said he would, because that is what you say on a campaign. However, I took the promise very seriously." After her husband won the election, Maathai established an employment agency to help the poor of Nairobi find work. Though her company never became very prosperous, she did manage to place quite a few people in jobs cleaning houses or planting trees and shrubs.

GREEN BELT MOVEMENT

Over time, Maathai became convinced that one of the best ways to help the people of Kenya was by protecting and improving their environment. As the population of Kenya increased, more and more trees were cut down to provide wood for fuel and building needs. This rapid removal of trees, or deforestation, caused the fertile topsoil that had once been anchored by tree roots to erode away. As the soil eroded, previously fertile areas turned into a barren desert—a process known as desertification.

Maathai recognized that the desertification of large parts of Kenya contributed to the problems of hunger and malnutrition among the nation's poor. For one thing, it made less land available for farming. For another, it meant that women had to walk long distances to gather firewood, so they were less likely to have time to cook hot, nutritious meals for their children. Maathai began thinking of ways to get Kenyan women interested and involved in reversing the trend toward desertification. "Because women here are responsible for their children, they cannot sit back, waste time and see them starve," she explained.

In 1977, Maathai acted on her concerns to form the Green Belt Movement, an organization of women that she hoped would plant trees throughout Kenya. "We started with seven trees in a small park in Nairobi," she recalled. "We had no nursery, no staff, and no funds, only a conviction that there was a role for ordinary country people in efforts to solve environmental problems." Before long, Maathai had gained the support of the National Council of Women of Kenya, and the Green Belt Movement expanded rapidly. "Soon, people from all over the country were asking us where they could find seedlings," she noted.

Green Belt employees—most of whom are women—plant seedlings in nurseries and care for them until they are ready to be transferred to local farms, schools, churches, and similar groups. The groups receive the trees for free, and the employees receive a small payment (about two cents) for each tree that survives for at least three months outside the nursery (the survival rate is between 50 and 80 percent, depending on the region). By the 1990s, the Green Belt Movement had 80,000 members and operated 1,500 nurseries. They have planted 10 million trees throughout Kenya and saved thousands of acres of topsoil. Thanks to this incredible level of success, the Green Belt Movement attracted the support of the United Nations and a number of European countries, as well as multinational corporations and individual donors. These financial resources helped expand the organization's annual budget to $5 million. The success of the Green Belt Movement also encouraged the formation of similar groups in a dozen other African countries.

Most importantly, according to Maathai, the Green Belt Movement had a positive effect on the lives of the women who participated. "The Green Belt Movement is about hope," she stated. "It tells people that they are responsible for their own lives. It suggests that at the very least, you can plant a tree and improve your habitat. It raises an awareness that people can take control of their environment, which is the first step toward greater participation in society."

The success of the Green Belt Movement did have one negative effect, however. As Maathai grew more prominent, some of her male colleagues, and even her own husband, began to resent her. "The typical African woman is supposed to be dependent, submissive, not better than her husband," she explained. In the early 1980s, the tension between Maathai and her husband resulted in an ugly divorce. Maathai was dragged into court and publicly accused of adultery, and she was shocked when the charge was upheld. "I told the judges that if they could reach that decision based on what they'd heard, they must be either incompetent or corrupt," she recalled. Angry about this comment, the judges sentenced Maathai to six months in jail. She was released after three days, however, when she agreed to apologize to the court.

Before long, Maathai experienced sexism again when she decided to run for Parliament. She took a leave of absence from her teaching position at the University of Nairobi in order to campaign, but she was prevented from becoming a candidate on a technicality. She believed that election officials were looking for any reason, no matter how questionable, to keep her out of the election. To make matters worse, the university blocked her attempts to return to her job afterward. At this time, Maathai began to realize what she was up against as a successful woman in Kenyan society. "I have had the fortune of breaking a lot of records—first woman this, first woman that—and I think that created a lot of jealousy without me realizing," she stated.

POLITICAL ACTIVISM

Maathai always believed that politics and the environment were closely related. For her environmental efforts to succeed in the long term, she felt that the Kenyan government needed to deal with the social and economic problems that plagued the people. "If we cannot protect our own species, I don't know what we are doing protecting the tree species," she noted.

Maathai became directly involved with politics in 1989, when she made enemies within Kenya's ruling party by opposing a major development

plan. President Daniel arap Moi wanted to build a 62-story skyscraper, accompanied by a huge statue of himself, in the middle of a popular park in downtown Nairobi. The proposed structure would cost the already financially strapped country $200 million, and would eliminate a major recreational area that many residents considered a refuge from urban life. "If I didn't react to their interfering with this central park, I may as well not plant another tree," Maathai explained. "I cannot condone that kind of activity and call myself an environmentalist."

Maathai called for public debate on the issue, and Nairobi residents responded by showering the government with letters of protest against the "park monster," as the proposed building came to be known. Faced with this public outcry, foreign investors withdrew their funds and the government was prevented from erecting the skyscraper. "Our children will not be condemned to the concrete jungle typical of the many unplanned, overcrowded, and polluted cities of other countries," Maathai stated.

Though Maathai was pleased with the outcome, it soon became clear that her campaign had made her very unpopular with the government. The Kenyan president said that her supporters had "insects in their heads" and claimed that it was "un-African and unimaginable for a woman to challenge or oppose men." One member of Parliament suggested putting a curse on Maathai, and another called her Green Belt Movement "subversive." Before long, her enemies in the ruling party ordered her to vacate the state-owned offices that the Green Belt Movement had occupied for 10 years, and effectively cut off the organization's funding by requiring contributions to go through the central government. Undaunted, Maathai moved the Green Belt headquarters to her home and made alternative funding arrangements with foreign investors.

As the political scene in Kenya became more turbulent in the 1990s, Maathai became even more active. Tired of the one-party dictatorship that had been in power since 1982, many people began calling for a return to democracy. In 1991, Maathai joined an opposition group known as the Forum for the Restoration of Democracy. Since then, she has often been harassed or detained by the police. In January 1992, she was arrested and charged with "malicious rumor-mongering and antigovernment speech," but the charges were not proved.

Later that year, Maathai was part of a group of women who went on a well-publicized hunger strike. They wanted to call attention to the government's unfair treatment of a group of political prisoners who had been held for two years without a trial. Many of the women were the mothers of the prisoners, and some were over 70 years old. After the peaceful protest had gone on for four days, police in riot gear surrounded the women, bombarding them with tear gas and beating them with clubs. Maathai was knocked unconscious and had to be hospitalized. "If nothing in the past would have brought the opposition together, these inhuman acts . . . surely must," she stated during a press conference following her release. "We call on the international community to view very seriously what is now happening."

As she became more politically active, Maathai realized that she also became a bigger target for her enemies. "I know I am in danger, and I know that the government has tried to put me aside," she admitted during a lecture tour in the United States. "At the moment, because of the political turmoil in my country, one cannot rule out the possibility of the worst, so I do feel that I need to take care of myself. I need to stay away from dangerous ground. But that doesn't mean that I will not go back home. I will go home because that is where I am needed most."

In early 1993, Maathai went to Rift Valley Province, an area of terrible ethnic violence in western Kenya, hoping to help end the conflict. While there, she learned that members of President Moi's ethnic group, the Kalenjin, were driving members of opposing tribes from their homes. She also uncovered evidence that the government was supporting the Kalenjin in various ways, including providing a police force that was sympathetic to their position and unlikely to intervene in their violent actions. Maathai explained that she got involved because "To me, here is a people who are displaced. I read about them. I see that their houses have been burned. I hear that their children are not going to school. I hear that they have been told to go back to their ancestral lands. . . . My response is to say, 'This is wrong. And the politicians must be stopped.' But I don't stop there. . . . I say, 'I'll stop them. If nobody's stopping them, I'll stop them.'" Toward this end, Maathai established the Tribal Clashes Resettlement Volunteer Service. The service helped the victims of ethnic violence organize in order to protect themselves and put greater pressure on the government to end the disputes.

SPREADING THE WORD

As her reputation as one of Africa's leading environmental and political activists has grown, Maathai has been in great demand around the world for lectures and interviews. These appearances have given her an opportunity to raise awareness in the international community. She often speaks out about how other nations contribute to the problems facing Africa. "For many leaders and decision makers in Africa, and throughout the world, development still means extensive farming of cash crops, expensive hydroelectric dams, hotels, supermarkets, and luxury items, which plunder human resourcefulness and natural resources. This is short-sighted and self-eliminating and does not meet the basic needs of the people — adequate food, clean water, shelter, local clinics, information, and freedom," she stated. "The tragic truth is that much of the continent is being impoverished by greedy and egocentric leaders assisted by international companies who take advantage of the fact that some presidents run their country as if it were their personal property. Oppressed, cowed, and living in debilitating poverty, the majority of Africans can only watch as their leaders mortgage them and their lands with projects they neither need nor want."

Given the success of the Green Belt Movement, however, Maathai remains hopeful for the future. "We must never lose hope," she noted. "When any of us feels she has an idea or an opportunity, she should go ahead and do it. I never knew when I was working in my backyard that what I was playing around with would someday become a whole movement. One person *can* make the difference."

MARRIAGE AND FAMILY

Maathai married a Kenyan businessman in the late 1960s. The marriage produced three children, but ended in divorce in the early 1980s. Maathai continues to live in Nairobi, Kenya, when she is not traveling the world to raise awareness of the problems facing her homeland.

WRITINGS

The Green Belt Movement, 1985
The Green Belt Movement: Sharing the Approach and the Experience, 1988

HONORS AND AWARDS

Woman of the Year Award: 1983
Right Livelihood Award: 1984
Award for the Protection of the Global Environment (Better World
    Society): 1986
Windstar Award for the Environment: 1988
Woman of the World Award: 1989
Africa Prize for Leadership for the Sustainable End to Hunger: 1991
Goldman Environmental Prize: 1991
Jane Addams Women's Leadership Award: 1993

FURTHER READING

BOOKS

Maathai, Wangari. *The Green Belt Movement*, 1985
——. *The Green Belt Movement: Sharing the Approach and the Experience*,
    1988
Wallace, Aubrey. *Eco-Heroes: Twelve Tales of Environmental Victory*, 1993
Who's Who in the World, 1996

PERIODICALS

Africa Report, Nov.-Dec. 1990, p.30
American Forests, Sep.-Oct. 1990, p.80
Chicago Tribune, Jan. 5, 1992, p.F1
Current Biography Yearbook 1993
Ms., Mar.-Apr. 1991, p.74; May-June 1992, p.10
Nation, Sep. 11, 1995, p.230
New York Times, Dec. 6, 1989, p.A4
Time, Apr. 23, 1990, p.80
Utne Reader, Nov.-Dec. 1992, p.86
Washington Post, June 2, 1992, p.D1

ADDRESS

Green Belt Movement
P.O. Box 67545
Nairobi, Kenya

Chico Mendes 1944-1988
Brazilian Labor Union Organizer and
Environmental Activist

BIRTH

Francisco "Chico" Alves Mendes Filho was born on December
15, 1944, near the jungle town of Xapuri, which is located in
Acre, a western province of Brazil. His father was a rubber
tapper (a person who gathers latex from rubber trees) named
Francisco Alves Mendes; his mother was Irâce Lopes Mendes.
Chico Mendes had many brothers and sisters—if they had all
lived to adulthood he would have had 17 siblings. The diffi-

cult circumstances of his family's life took their toll, however. By the time Mendes was grown, only six of his brothers and sisters were still alive.

YOUTH

Mendes's childhood was marked by long days of hard work deep in Brazil's Amazon rainforest. The people who lived in the region—whether rubber tappers employed by wealthy estate owners or native Indians—were very poor and isolated, and parents often struggled to feed and clothe their children. In addition, many aspects of their lives were controlled by the rich people who owned the land where they lived and worked. As Andrew Revkin noted in *The Burning Season,* the Amazon region in which the rubber tappers lived was "humid, dark, closed—an insect-ridden wilderness. Disease was rampant. There were no hospitals, no schools. Even though Brazil had been collecting millions of dollars in taxes on the harvested rubber, the government had put nothing back into the region. Every aspect of life presented a new challenge. Families were dispersed throughout the forest, often separated by four- or five-mile hikes. Isolation required self-sufficiency, so each family hunted and gathered what could not be grown or bought from the traveling merchants."

Faced with such a harsh environment, children often had to take on many hard chores at a very early age, and Mendes and his brothers and sisters were no exception. It was especially important for the children of the Mendes family to help out, for their father suffered from club feet, a deformity that made it hard for him to get around.

By the time Mendes was five years old, he was spending long hours of every day collecting firewood and hauling big pots of water. A few years later, he accompanied his father into the forest, where he was taught how to drain the latex out of the rubber trees that towered all around them. Francisco Mendes also pointed out the dangers and complexity of the wild rainforest to the young boy, and he developed an appreciation and respect for the world's natural wonders. "I became an ecologist long before I had ever heard the word," Mendes remarked many years later.

Chico Mendes also learned to read and write from his father, who was one of the few literate tappers in the province. "The rubber estate owners would not allow schools," Mendes later explained, "because if a rubber tapper's children went to school, they would learn to read, write, and add up—and then they would discover to what extent they were being cheated." Mendes was determined to learn to read, though, and his father was happy to tutor him. On some nights, the entire Mendes household would be silent except for the low murmur of Francisco Mendes's voice as he read to young Chico by the smoky light of a lone oil lamp. By the time he was 11 years old, Mendes was known in the region as a very bright boy, even though he was by all accounts somewhat odd-looking. Revkin noted that one friend of the Mendes family recalled how, when Mendes was a youngster, "you'd never have thought that Chico could grow up into such a man. He used to walk around with his mouth hanging open, and he drooled. But he fooled you. Everyone admired how such a small kid could read so fluently."

EDUCATION

When Mendes was a teenager, he and his family moved to a region of eastern Acre known as Cachoeira. In 1956, several months after the move, a stranger showed up at the family's home. The stranger struck up a conversation with Mendes and his father, who quickly recognized that the man was extremely knowledgeable about politics, literature, and other aspects of life outside of the Amazon Basin. Chico Mendes and his father paid a few visits to the man over the next several weeks, and each visit seemed to confirm their initial impression that the mysterious stranger was a very well-educated fellow.

Before long the man was acting as Mendes's teacher; as Revkin wrote, "the man was clearly a loner, [but] something in Chico's attitude—and possibly his being one of the few youngsters who had already learned the rudiments of reading—convinced him to work with this youth. None of the other children on the *seringal* (rubber-tapping estate) interested the man, and he interested none of them."

Months later, the stranger finally took Mendes into his confidence. He identified himself as Euclides Fernandes Tavora, a military officer from a wealthy Brazilian family who had escaped from prison after taking part in a failed coup attempt against Getulio Vargas, the ruler of the country at the time. Tavora told Mendes that he had joined in the attempt because he had become so sickened by the widening gap between rich and poor in their country. Given the teenager's already great admiration for Tavora, this information undoubtedly had a big impact on Mendes.

By the early 1960s Mendes had learned a great deal about the vast world that loomed beyond the rainforest. He continued to spend a great deal of time with Tavora, talking about political issues and listening to radio broadcasts from Voice of America, Radio Moscow, and the British Broadcasting Service (BBC). "He would explain the news and tell me about the struggles of workers all over the world," said Mendes. In 1966 Tavora died from a mysterious stomach ailment, and Mendes mourned the loss of his long-time friend and mentor.

CAREER HIGHLIGHTS

During the mid-1960s Mendes taught other rubber tappers in Acre how to read, and he wrote a number of letters to authorities in which he complained about the unfair treatment that rubber tappers received at the hands of the wealthy land owners. His letters were ignored, though, and the situation soon worsened.

In 1964 Brazil's military staged a successful coup against the government and installed their own leaders as the country's rulers. The military was determined to relieve crowded conditions in Brazilian cities and exploit the resources of the Amazon for economic gain, so they encouraged settlers and wealthy ranchers and farmers to go and tame the rainforest. Many of these people cleared the land by cutting or setting fire to the forest. These practices horrified the Indians and rubber tappers who relied on the forest for their livelihood, but they had no political power, so they were helpless to stop the destruction.

"By encouraging the fastest possible development of the frontier, the Brazilian government essentially forced the scattered inhabitants of the rainforest to pay the price of deforestation—ranging from air pollution to the spread of disease to flooding and soil erosion—while a few wealthy landowners reaped most of the rewards," wrote Aaron Sachs in the *Humanist*. The practices of the newcomers angered and worried Mendes, and he launched his first efforts to organize the rubber tappers into a union in the late 1960s. He knew that if he could unify the rubber tappers into one strong organization, their voices would be harder for the government to ignore.

ORGANIZING A UNION

In 1971 Mendes moved to Xapuri to pursue his interest in union organizing and politics. As destruction of the Amazon rainforest continued, enthusiasm for a rubber tappers union blossomed, nourished by the Catholic church and organizers like Joao Maia. In 1975 a union was formally established, and Mendes was elected to the group's leadership. Other unions formed across the region as well, and the rubber tappers embarked on a movement based on acts of peaceful resistance.

Over the next few years Mendes and the other union leaders lobbied the government to halt the destruction of the rainforest and to provide funding for schools and hospitals. They also led several successful *empates* (protests) in which they were able to protect large sections of the Amazon from the ranchers who wanted to clear it for rangeland. Some observers estimate that these protests saved up to three million acres of forest over the years.

The wealthy ranchers were infuriated by the unions' actions, and their hatred of Mendes and other union leaders quickly reached dangerous levels. In early 1980 four masked men severely beat Mendes, and seven months later, union president Wilson Pinheiro was murdered by thugs who had been hired by the ranchers. The ranchers may have thought that Pinheiro's death would convince the unions to drop their opposition, but instead the murder galvanized union members. A rancher who was known to have been involved in ordering Pinheiro's death was subsequently killed, and the police — who had not bothered with an investigation after the union leader's murder — arrested and tortured many rubber tappers in an unsuccessful effort to find out who had killed the rancher.

In the 1980s tensions between the rubber tappers and the ranchers continued to escalate. Mendes and the other union leaders established schools and education programs, and the rubber tapper movement continued to grow. In 1985 the rubber tappers of the Amazon united under the banner of the Conselho Nacional dos Seringueiros (National Council of Rubber Tappers), and they began to work together with the Indians of the Amazon. "The struggle of the Indians should be the same as the fight of the rubber tappers," said Mendes. "We are not each other's enemies. We should fight together to defend our Amazon."

Mendes also became acquainted with a number of people outside of Brazil who were supportive of his efforts during the early 1980s. People such as filmmaker Adrian Cowell, environmental activist Jose Lutzenberger, and Institute for Amazonian Studies director Mary Helena Allegretti "took Mendes to boardrooms, banks, and Congress [during the 1980s]," wrote Tom Mathews in *Newsweek*. "Their lobbying, fund-raising and media-manipulating skills gave him an audience far beyond the forest."

ENVIRONMENTAL ISSUES

By the mid-1980s Mendes and his allies were wielding a new weapon in their fight to save the Amazon: environmental concerns. The long years of cutting and burning the rainforest had decimated large stretches of the Amazon, destroying its natural beauty, ruining the habitat of countless animals, and wrecking the lives of many rural people who had used the resources of the forest without obliterating it. In addition, growing numbers of scientists proclaimed that the fires in the Amazon were major factors in air pollution and global warming. "The burning of the Amazon was no longer a regional but a global problem," wrote Revkin. "Even for those who doubted the value of preserving a great reservoir of genetic wealth, there was something startling about fires so vast that they emitted more pollutants than the industrial complexes of West Germany and Poland combined."

Mendes joined forces with environmental organizations in the United States and Brazil to publicize the terrible damage that had been done to the rainforest over the previous two decades. They prepared reports showing

how sensible extraction of rainforest resources could help Brazil's economy and how only a few people were benefiting from current policies. Working together, Mendes and his allies convinced international banking organizations to suspend their financial support for highways and other projects that would further damage the rainforest. Faced with growing domestic unrest and international outrage, the Brazilian government finally began to re-examine some of its Amazon policies.

The activists who worked with Mendes marveled over his talent and his dedication. "He was the person who could round people up and get them talking," wrote Revkin. "More important, he could get them to act. Everyone who worked with him said over and over that Mendes was not doing what he did for power, glory, or money—which some others among the leadership of the tapper movement were sometimes accused of—but simply because he felt so strongly that it had to be done."

By 1987 Mendes was known around the world for his efforts to stop the destruction of the rainforest. He received awards from the United Nations and the Better World Society for his tireless efforts, and environmental groups hailed him as one of the natural world's great defenders. Mendes, though, was always quick to point out that while it was important to protect the Amazon and the animals that lived within it, he was most concerned with helping the poor people who struggled to support their families in the face of violence, pollution, and poverty. "There are thousands of people living [in the Amazon] who depend on the forest—and their lives are in danger every day," he said.

DANGEROUS FIGHT

Mendes persevered in his efforts even though he received many death threats. He stayed with his people in Xapuri, which remained very isolated. Friends and families sometimes tried to convince him to leave for a safer place, but he always refused, saying "I would be a coward to do this. My blood is the same blood as that of these people suffering here. I can't run. There's something inside me that cannot leave here. This is the place where I will finish my mission."

Indeed, Mendes made sure that everyone knew how proud he was to be a part of the rainforest community. "I am a rubber tapper," he said in one speech. "My people have lived in the forest for over 130 years, using its resources without destroying it. We appeal to the American people to help us. Together, we can preserve the forest and make it productive. We can secure this immense treasure for the future of all our children."

In 1988 Mendes and the other rubber tappers scored several significant victories. They saved important sections of rainforest, and they even managed to drive two frustrated cattle barons out of the region entirely. Rancher Darly Alves da Silva and his family remained, though, and as the months passed, rumors began to fly that the Alves clan, which had a reputation for violence and brutality, was planning on killing the activist.

On December 22, 1988, Mendes was killed by a shotgun blast outside his home in Xapuri. His death sent shock waves throughout Brazil and the international community. His funeral was held on Christmas Day, and thousands of rubber tappers hiked over miles of rough terrain to reach the town and pay their respects to the man who had worked so hard on their behalf. Human rights activists and environmental leaders from around the world sent their condolences as well, for they recognized that they had lost one of their most talented and principled leaders.

A few days after Mendes was murdered, Darly Alves da Silva and his son Darcy were arrested for the killing. In December 1990 they were each convicted and sentenced to 19-year prison terms. In 1993 the two men escaped from prison. The father was recaptured in July 1996, but his son remains at large.

The death of their leader, meanwhile, only encouraged the rubber tappers and their supporters to fight harder against those who threatened the Amazon rainforest. "When Mendes died, the chain-saw-mad landowners in the Amazon gloated," wrote Geri Smith in *U.S. News & World Report.* They originally thought that the loss of Mendes would make it easier for them to take what they wanted. Instead, the defenders of the rainforest vowed that their leader's death would not be in vain. As one of his many friends said during the funeral, "Chico is alive in the things that he did, the things that he stood for. Our commitment is to proceed with the fight." In recognition of Mendes's social and environmental activism, Brazil set aside about 2.4 million acres of protected rainforest as the Chico Mendes Extractive Reserve.

MARRIAGE AND FAMILY

Mendes married Maria Eunice Feitosa on February 7, 1969. The marriage was troubled from the beginning, though, and his long absences on union business further hurt the relationship. They had one child, Angela, before they divorced. In April 1983 he married again, wedding Ilzamar Gadelha Bezerra, a young woman whom he had tutored when she was a child. They had a daughter, Elenira, and a son, Sandino, before his death.

WRITINGS

Fight for the Forest: Chico Mendes in His Own Words, 1989 (interviews)

HONORS AND AWARDS

Global 500 Award (United Nations): 1987
Protection of the Environment Medal (Better World Society): 1987

FURTHER READING

BOOKS

Cowell, Adrian. *The Decade of Destruction: The Crusade to Save the Amazon Rain Forest,* 1990

DeStefano, Susan. *Chico Mendes: Fight for the Forest,* 1992 (juvenile)

Hecht, Susanna, and Alexander Cockburn. *The Fate of the Forest: Developers, Destroyers, and Defenders of the Amazon,* 1989

Mendes, Chico. *Fight for the Forest: Chico Mendes in His Own Words,* 1989 (interviews)

Revkin, Andrew. *The Burning Season: The Murder of Chico Mendes and the Fight for the Amazon Rain Forest,* 1990

Shoumatoff, Alex. *The World Is Burning,* 1990

PERIODICALS

Discover, Jan. 1990, p.30
The Economist, Jan. 7, 1989, p.36
Humanist, Mar./Apr. 1996, p.5
Interview, Apr. 1989, p.62
Maclean's, Dec. 24, 1990, p.17
The Nation, Apr. 1, 1991, p.410
New York Times, Aug. 12, 1988, p.A1; Dec. 24, 1988, p.A1; July 2, 1996, p.A2
Newsweek, Sep. 3, 1990, p.62
People, Jan. 15, 1990, p.28
Time, Jan. 9, 1989, p.38; Dec. 24, 1990, p.45
TV Guide, Sep. 24, 1994, p.26
U.S. News & World Report, Dec. 24, 1990, p.18

Russell A. Mittermeier 1949-
American Conservationist, Primatologist, and Herpetologist
President of Conservation International

BIRTH

Russell Alan Mittermeier was born in New York City on November 8, 1949. He was the only child of Francis Xavier Mittermeier, a stamp dealer, and Bertha Mittermeier, a homemaker. Both his parents had immigrated to the United States from Germany before he was born, and he grew up speaking both German and English.

YOUTH

Until Mittermeier was nine years old, his family lived within the boundaries of New York City, spending seven years in the Bronx and two years in Brooklyn. During this time, Mittermeier often explored the city with his mother, routinely visiting the Bronx Zoo and the American Museum of Natural History. He was fascinated with animals from an early age, and he loved both seeing them at the zoo and hearing stories about them at bedtime, when his mother read him "jungle books" that described untamed lands filled with adventure. When he was just six years old, Mittermeier told his first-grade teacher that he wanted to be a "jungle explorer."

In 1958, the Mittermeier family moved to the rural setting of North Babylon, Long Island. Suddenly Mittermeier could experience nature firsthand, and he spent hours foraging through the forests and swamps near his home. His parents allowed him to make a giant turtle pond in the backyard, where he always kept dozens of turtles that he found around his neighborhood. In the family den, Mittermeier installed 20 fish tanks to hold his collection of snakes and lizards, which included not only the native species that he found in local swamps but also some varieties that were not from the area. He fondly referred to his creatures as "herps," from the word "herpetology," which is the study of reptiles and amphibians.

By the time Mittermeier had reached the eighth grade, he had read Edgar Rice Burroughs's Tarzan books and knew with certainty what he wanted to do when he grew up. "I was never really interested in being anything other than a wildlife biologist," he explained. "I read all of the Edgar Rice Burroughs books and something clicked with me." There is no doubt that wallowing around in the swamplands of Long Island prepared him for his adult job of searching the jungles of the world. "I got very used to having things like leeches hanging on me and rolling around in the mud, which is a very basic part of fieldwork in the tropics," he noted. "Collecting 'herps' when I was little gave me a good eye for snakes, and that's really an important thing when you're working in the tropics, to be able to see things like poisonous snakes. I've never had any trouble with them because I have sort of an instinct for spotting snakes."

By the age of 16, Mittermeier's deep love and appreciation for the outdoors led him to become active in protecting the environment. In the late 1950s and early 1960s, Long Island experienced an explosion of growth. Many of Mittermeier's favorite swamps were swallowed up by land developers and paved over for shopping malls. In response to this destruction of animal habitat, Mittermeier helped found the Long Island Herpetological Society to educate the residents of Long Island about the loss of local wilderness areas. During high school, he wrote many articles for the society's journal stressing the importance of protecting native wildlife.

EDUCATION

Mittermeier was always a good student, and he graduated second in his class from North Babylon High School in 1967. In addition to his excellent grades, Mittermeier made his mark in high school as editor of the school newspaper and star of the track and field team. He set up homemade high jump and pole vault equipment in his backyard, next to his turtle pond, and during his teen years he could often be found outside practicing these events or running around the neighborhood.

Mittermeier earned a scholarship to attend Dartmouth College in Hanover, New Hampshire. He started out as a biology major, but he soon found that the biology courses were intended mainly for students who wanted to become medical doctors. He switched his major to zoology and soon had taken all the courses offered by the department of anthropology. Mittermeier spent several semesters of college studying wildlife in other countries, and it was during this time that he discovered his love of primates, a classification of animals that includes gorillas, chimpanzees, baboons, and lemurs. He spent his senior year on Barro Colorado Island, off the Panama Canal in Central America, studying the ecology and behavior of the neotropical primates native to this region. His honors thesis on the subject of neotropical primates, which incorporated his own findings as well as research he had done on the work of other scientists, was more than 300 pages long. Mittermeier graduated from Dartmouth in 1971, earning his bachelor's degree with highest honors.

During his years at Dartmouth, Mittermeier had attended a lecture given by Irven DeVore, a famous scientist in the study of primates who taught at Harvard University in Massachusetts. After speaking with Mittermeier, DeVore was impressed by the young man's wealth of knowledge and field experience and encouraged him to pursue his graduate school education at Harvard. Eager to follow this advice, Mittermeier enrolled as a student in Harvard's department of biological anthropology, which focused on the study of biological aspects of human evolution. While there, Mittermeier continued to impress people with his passion for learning and his independent spirit. "Probably the Harvard faculty had less influence on Russ than almost anyone I have known since I came to Harvard," DeVore recalled. "He knew what he wanted to do, and he knew what he wanted each of us to do for him."

Mittermeier continued his jungle explorations during graduate school, when he made his first important discovery. When he was 24 years old, he went on a 12-day expedition in the South American country of Peru with two friends. While traveling deep in the tropical rain forest they came across a Peruvian yellow-tailed woolly monkey, an extremely rare species that was formerly believed to be extinct.

During his Harvard years, Mittermeier spent almost half of his time doing field research on primates in exotic locations like Suriname, Panama, Mexico, Tanzania, and Brazil. His wonderful experiences with jungle primates led him to specialize in the field of primatology, and also earned him the nickname "Russell of the Apes." Mittermeier earned his master's degree from Harvard in 1973, and he received his doctoral degree four years later. His 800-page doctoral thesis—which DeVore said was the most comprehensive he had seen in 20 years at Harvard—was an in-depth study of the monkeys of Suriname, a small country on the Atlantic coast of South America. In all this time, Mittermeier always maintained his interest in reptiles, and he even discovered three new species of turtles.

CAREER HIGHLIGHTS

CREATING THE ROLE OF "BIOPOLITICIAN"

When Mittermeier graduated from Harvard, he had already published almost 50 scientific papers and chapters in books—an almost unheard of accomplishment for a scientist at the beginning of his career. He had also made several important primate discoveries. But instead of just continuing his field studies of primates and reptiles, Mittermeier also began making a name for himself as a prominent conservationist. His dynamic personality and passionate belief that he could change the world led him to create a unique career for himself as a "biopolitician," combining field research with highly visible social and political crusades in order to protect the endangered animals and forests of the world.

"I think it had to do with my personality type," Mittermeier explained about his career choice, describing himself as a person with "a strong biological background . . . who can also engage in the politics and diplomacy that make up so much of conservation." One of his colleagues noted that Mittermeier "has the kinds of skills that a modern-day conservationist needs but very few of them have. He is equally at home up to his knees in the rain forest or in a board room in Washington." His mentor Professor DeVore added that "in a certain sense he carved out his own niche: he conceived of what needed to be done and set out to do it."

Mittermeier began his career as a conservation associate with the New York Zoological Society in 1976. A year later, he became a conservation fellow in primate ecology with the World Wildlife Fund. Before long he became the head of the World Wildlife Fund's primate program, a position he held for the next 10 years. Since the nature of Mittermeier's professional responsibilities allowed him to hold several positions simultaneously, he also served as an adviser for the Species Survival Commission (SSC) of the International Union for the Conservation of Nature and Natural Resources. In 1977, he was appointed chairman of the SSC's Primate Specialist Group. Within the same year, Mittermeier published his first major work on conservation, a 300-page book entitled *Global Strategy for Primate Conservation.* This work, which looks at primate conservation issues on a worldwide basis, presents specific "action plans" to preserve some of the world's endangered animal and plant species.

Since then, Mittermeier has often used the written word to express his views and to communicate with his fellow scientists. In 1981, he started a newsletter for the Primate Specialist Group, *Primate Conservation,* which has become an international forum for the exchange of new information among the world's primate conservationists. In this same year, Mittermeier edited and contributed to the first volume of another important international series, entitled *Ecology and Behavior of Neotropical Primates.* Some of his later works include *Primate Conservation in the Tropical Rain Forest* (1987) and *The Lemurs of Madagascar: An Action Plan for Their Conservation, 1993-1999* (1992), as well as numerous articles in popular magazines and scientific journals.

SAVING THE MURIQUI MONKEY IN BRAZIL

Mittermeier's fight to save the endangered muriqui monkey in Brazil provides an excellent example of his role as "biopolitician." A few hundred years ago, before the human population in Brazil exploded, it is estimated that there were about 400,000 muriqui monkeys in the wild. By the 1990s, however, there were only 400 to 500 left. The muriqui lives only in the Atlantic forest region of eastern Brazil, which used to be an expanse of untouched land about the size of California and Texas combined. Over the past hundred years, however, the major cities of Sao Paulo and Rio de Janeiro have developed in this region, so only about two percent of the original rain forest remains.

In his crusade to save the muriqui, Mittermeier gave the Brazilians a sense of pride in their native forests. He sponsored an enormous advertising campaign that used the muriqui as a "flagship species," so pictures of the cute little monkey appeared throughout Brazil—on posters, postage stamps, T-shirts, bumper stickers, telephone book covers, and corporate logos. Before this time, few residents of Brazil realized that their country housed many endangered monkey species that did not exist anywhere else in the world. "People often don't realize that they have a unique species in their country," he noted. "They're surprised we don't have them in America." Mittermeier's work raised public awareness and led large numbers of average Brazilians to support the drastic steps that were necessary to save the monkeys from extinction. As a result, he explained, "the muriqui has become the symbol of the Brazilian conservation movement, as visible and popular as the panda is in China."

In 1982, Mittermeier acted as the field coordinator and producer of a film called *The Cry of the Muriqui,* which told the world about the sad fate of many of Brazil's primate species. In 1989, in another example of what he called his "unorthodox approach to getting the word out," Mittermeier posed for an advertisement for the Gap clothing store chain holding a tiny, white-faced capuchin monkey. "It's more important to be published in *Elle* or *Esquire* or even *Road and Track* than in natural-history magazines," he noted, "because we're getting to a new audience. We're getting more people to the cause."

SERVING AS PRESIDENT OF CONSERVATION INTERNATIONAL

In 1989, Mittermeier became president of a newly formed conservation group called Conservation International (CI). The group's motto, which seems particularly appropriate for Mittermeier, is "Heads in the sky, feet in the mud." The goal of CI has been to identify environmental "hot spots" on the planet—areas that are the most biologically diverse and at the same time the most endangered—and to create social and political action plans to save them. In the next 20 or 30 years, it is projected that one-fourth of the total plant and animal species in the world will become extinct. Three-fourths of the earth's species live in tropical rain forest regions, which are being eliminated at a rate of 27 million acres (an area about the size of New York State) per year. Many rain forests are located in poor, developing countries in South America, Asia, and Africa. The trees that are removed are sold as timber to provide income to local people or to enrich the country's wealthy elite, and the land that is cleared is often turned into farms.

CI takes each region's economy and native culture into account when developing strategies to save the tropical rain forests. Mittermeier has been involved in many innovative CI projects aimed at enhancing local conservation efforts. In one project, called a "debt-for-nature swap," the national debt of a Third World country is partially eliminated in exchange for an environmental commitment from that country. Other projects attempt to make threatened areas more valuable in their natural state than they would be if they were developed. The Tagua Initiative, for example, created a new industry for Ecuador by harvesting the tagua nut, ivorylike in appearance, for use as buttons in the American clothing industry. Since the nuts have commercial value, the trees are protected. The Seed Ventures Program also protects trees by seeking out other nontimber products that can be marketed to support local economies. Helping to coordinate all these CI activities is the Geographic Information System, which utilizes computer technology to map and plan conservation efforts.

In his role as "biopolitician," Mittermeier has played a key role in the success of CI. His ability to speak seven languages fluently allows him to become "a citizen of wherever he is," according to one colleague. Since he fits right into the cultures of the areas he visits, Mittermeier is able to work closely with local people to gain their acceptance for his ideas and projects. "He understands and respects the culture of the people in the country he goes to. There's no arrogance to him," another colleague commented. Mittermeier explained that his goal as president of CI was "to be able to look back someday and see that the course of conservation history changed because of our efforts."

In addition to his work for CI, Mittermeier promotes conservation issues by attending international meetings, making lecture and fundraising tours throughout the world, teaching courses at the State University of New York at Stony Brook, and publishing numerous articles. Despite his hectic schedule, he still manages to spend at least two months per year in the jungle. On some of his solo excursions, he has been known to bring along just a machete, a hammock, and a few cans of tuna. Though he has had a few close calls, including coming within an arm's length of a jaguar, Mittermeier claimed that the excitement of exploring jungles was well worth the risk. "Sure there's an element of danger, but the key thing is that every day there's a chance that you'll find something no one has ever observed before," he explained.

VIEWS ON CONSERVATION

"Conservation of biological diversity should be a fundamental human preoccupation, and I intend to do everything possible, both individually and institutionally, to bring this about," Mittermeier stated. "If we don't make the same level of emotional and financial commitment to conservation in the nineties that we made to the space program in the sixties, our children and grandchildren are destined to inhabit a world that is biologically more impoverished than the world into which we were born. And that is what [I am] committed to preventing." Despite the many threats to the earth's environment, Mittermeier remained optimistic. "We simply have to approach conservation as the art of the possible, and if we do that I see no reason why we can't turn today's conservation dreams into tomorrow's conservation reality," he stated.

MARRIAGE AND FAMILY

On July 4, 1984, Mittermeier married Isabel Constable, a biologist. They had one son, John, before they were divorced in 1989. Two years later Mittermeier married Cristina Goettsch, a member of the CI staff in Mexico. They also had a son, Michael. When he is not traveling, Mittermeier lives with his family in a semirural area of Great Falls, Virginia. Their home is filled with tribal art that he has collected from all over the world, as well as books on natural history and wildlife prints of primates and turtles.

HOBBIES AND OTHER INTERESTS

To stay in top physical condition for his excursions into the jungle, Mittermeier runs, lifts weights, swims, canoes, and plays basketball regularly.

SELECTED WRITINGS

Global Strategy for Primate Conservation, 1977
Primate Conservation in the Tropical Rain Forest, 1987*Conservation Action Plan for Suriname,* 1990
Lemurs of Madagascar: An Action Plan for Their Conservation, 1993-1999, 1992

HONORS AND AWARDS

San Diego Zoological Society Gold Medal: 1988

FURTHER READING

PERIODICALS

Audubon, Jan.-Feb. 1992, p.90
Current Biography Yearbook 1992
Environment, Apr. 1990, p.16
International Wildlife, Jan.-Feb. 1997, p.12
New York Times Magazine, Sep. 22, 1996, p.98
People, Nov. 28, 1988, p.165
St. Louis Post-Dispatch, July 24, 1990, p.D1
Smithsonian, Dec. 1985, p.100
Washingtonian, Nov. 1991, p.80

ADDRESS

Conservation International
1015 18th St. NW
Suite 1000
Washington, D.C. 20036

WORLD WIDE WEB SITE

http://www.conservation.org

Margaret Murie 1902-
Olaus J. Murie 1889-1963
American Authors and Conservationists
Founding Members of the Wilderness
Society
Leaders in Fight to Create Arctic National
Wildlife Refuge in Alaska

BIRTH

MARGARET

Margaret Elizabeth Thomas Murie, known from childhood by
the nickname "Mardy," was born on August 18, 1902, in

Seattle, Washington. Her parents divorced when she was very young, so Margaret was raised by her mother, Minnie, and her stepfather, Louis Gillette, who was an attorney. She had two half-sisters, Louise and Carol, and a half-brother, Louis.

OLAUS

Olaus Johan Murie was born on March 1, 1889, on a small farm near Moorhead, Minnesota. His parents had immigrated to the United States from Norway just a year before his birth. He had two brothers, one of whom (Adolph Murie) also became a prominent conservationist and writer.

YOUTH

MARGARET

When Margaret was nine years old, her family moved to Fairbanks, Alaska, where her stepfather became an assistant U.S. attorney. At that time, Alaska was not yet a state and Fairbanks was a rugged, isolated frontier town. As Margaret described it, Fairbanks in those days consisted of "a flat patter of hodgepodge buildings and low log cabins, smoke plumes rising straight up from all the little iron stovepipes defying the cold and loneliness and all the powers of the unbeatable North." Although it was a challenge to keep their four-room cabin warm when the temperatures reached 50 degrees below zero, the family adapted well to life in Alaska.

As a girl, Margaret loved to explore the countryside near her home—by dogsled in the winter and on foot in the summer. From her earliest days in the Far North, she gained a deep appreciation for wilderness. "Alaska is indeed indescribable," she wrote later. "Words cannot tell it. Pictures help—but they cannot convey the sense of space, the silence and the sounds, the sounds that belong there: bird song, wolf song, river song. And the air, the skies, the endless light of summer, the soft dark of winter."

OLAUS

Olaus's father died when he was very young, so he and his brothers had to work hard throughout their childhood to help support the family. Olaus milked the family cow before and after school, cut firewood in the forest and dragged it home on his little sled, and helped the neighbors plow their fields. Despite the hardship, however, he still enjoyed his childhood years in rural Minnesota—especially time spent swimming or camping out in the woods. One summer he built a canoe with his brothers and paddled it up and down the Red River near their home.

EDUCATION

MARGARET

Margaret recalled that during her school years in rural Alaska, all the children got the day off when the first flowers bloomed in the spring. Since there were no colleges in Alaska when she graduated from high school in 1919, Margaret had to travel nine days by horse-drawn sleigh to attend Reed College in Portland, Oregon. After two years of studying to be a teacher, though, she changed her mind and returned home to Fairbanks. In 1921, she moved to Boston, where she attended Simmons College for a year. By the time she came back to Alaska, the University of Alaska at Fairbanks had opened and begun accepting students. Margaret enrolled during the second year that the college existed. She earned her bachelor's degree in business administration in 1924, becoming the first woman graduate of the school.

OLAUS

During his school days in Minnesota, Olaus always loved to draw. He showed such artistic talent that his eighth-grade teacher pulled him aside on the last day of school and made him promise to keep on drawing. After graduating from high school, Olaus studied biology at Fargo College in North Dakota for a few years. When his favorite professor moved to Pacific University in Oregon, Olaus followed, earning his bachelor's degree in biology there in 1912.

CAREER HIGHLIGHTS

OLAUS IN THE FIELD

After he graduated from Pacific University, Olaus spent two years working for the Oregon state game warden, photographing and collecting specimens of wildlife. In 1914, he quit to become a field biologist for the Carnegie Museum. Though the museum itself was located in Pittsburgh, Olaus spent most of his time on expeditions to remote areas studying wildlife. One of his early trips took him to Hudson Bay in northern Canada. He and another scientist, using Ojibway Indians as guides, traveled through the frigid waters in canoes and collected animal specimens from uncharted islands. Despite the danger involved, Olaus considered it a great adventure and fell in love with the Arctic wilderness. He led another expedition to Baffin Island in 1917. In all of his field work, Olaus brought along his sketchbook and made detailed drawings of the land and animals he studied.

During World War II, Olaus joined the U.S. Army and served overseas as an observer with the balloon service. Upon his return in 1920, he took a job

109

with the U.S. Biological Survey (now called the U.S. Fish and Wildlife Service) in Alaska. At that time, much of Alaska was still unexplored, and little was known about the animals that lived there. Olaus traveled all around the vast tundra—by dogsled, in a canoe, or on snowshoes—studying various kinds of wildlife, including caribou, grizzly bears, and waterfowl.

THE MURIES
BECOME A TEAM

In 1921, shortly after Olaus had moved to Alaska, he and Margaret met at the home of a mutual friend. They took a boat ride together later that evening, and Margaret was impressed when Olaus exchanged a series of hoots with an owl. Olaus's work kept him away from Fairbanks for the next year, but when he and Margaret met again their friendship grew into a serious romantic relationship. They were married in an old mission church near the Yukon River in 1924, just after Margaret had graduated from college.

Immediately after the wedding, Margaret joined Olaus on an expedition to study the migration and mating patterns of Alaska's 150,000-member Porcupine Caribou herd. At first the Muries lived in a one-room log cabin in Bettles, Alaska, while they waited for the land and water to freeze so they could continue north. Then they embarked on a 10-week journey by dogsled into the Endicott Mountains, north of the Arctic Circle. Before long, Margaret learned to make careful scientific observations and became a valuable assistant to Olaus. When they returned to civilization, Margaret found that she had been changed by the experience. "If you're living in some untouched area, some wilderness, you just can't go off and forget it," she stated. "It does something to you."

In 1925, Margaret went to stay with her parents in Washington to have the Muries' first child, Martin. She and Olaus both found it difficult to be apart, however, so from then on their whole family, which soon grew to include two more children, Joanne and Donald, went on expeditions together. Though some people said that it was not safe to take young children into the wilderness, Margaret noted that her kids "grew and were brown and never had a sick moment that I can recall. Their play was no problem: they were busy from morning till night with places and objects they found right in the wilderness." Many years later, Margaret wrote a book, *Two in the Far North*, about her experiences raising a family in rural Alaska.

After he had worked in the field for many years, Olaus decided to continue his education. He moved the family to Michigan, where he received his master's degree in biology from the University of Michigan in 1927. Later that year, the Murie family moved to Moose, Wyoming, near Jackson Hole. The government had hired Olaus as a consultant to find out why the elk herd that lived in the nearby Teton Mountains had been dying off. As before, the whole family accompanied him on research trips, riding on horseback into the mountains to study the elk. Their work revealed that the elk were suffering because of the activities of cattle ranchers in the area. Cattle had taken over much of the land that the elk depended on for food and forced the herd higher into the mountains, where food was less abundant. In addition, some ranchers had adopted a policy of killing the elk's natural predators, such as wolves and mountain lions, because they worried that these animals would harm their cattle. The resulting imbalance in the predator-prey relationship led to a weaker elk herd. Olaus recommended expanding the size of the wildlife refuge that was set aside for the elk. When his ideas were implemented, the herd soon began to recover. Years later he published the results of his landmark study in *The Elk of North America*.

THE FIGHT TO PRESERVE WILDERNESS

As the Muries learned more about the threats that human intervention posed to animals and their habitat, they became increasingly active in the fight to protect wilderness. Before long, their home in Wyoming became a gathering place for people interested in conservation issues. In 1935, Olaus founded an environmental organization called the Wilderness Society with Robert Marshall and other activists. The group's main goal was to secure government protection for as much of the remaining North American wilderness as possible. "For those of us who feel something is missing unless we can hike across land disturbed only by our footsteps or see creatures roaming freely as they have always done, we are sure there should still be wilderness," Margaret explained.

Olaus retired from government service in 1945 and became a director of the Wilderness Society. Margaret called herself his secretary, but in fact she was just as involved in conservation issues as her husband. In those days, just after World War II, the United States was experiencing a rapid boom in construction. Often the new developments took over land that was previously inhabited by wildlife. The Muries gave lectures all over the country about the importance of preserving wilderness. Olaus was elected president of the Wilderness Society in 1950 and served in that position for the next seven years.

Having lived in Alaska for many years, the Muries had a special interest in protecting its large areas of wilderness. In 1956, they led an expedition to the Brooks Range in northeastern Alaska to record the ecological changes that had taken place as a result of human intervention, such as building towns and mining for minerals. Their studies revealed that wildlife was being harmed by increased human activity in the region. In response, the Muries led an effort to convince the federal government to create a wildlife refuge to protect large areas of Alaskan wilderness. "Alaska is the last treasure of wilderness that we'll ever have," Margaret noted. "I think we need to be very careful about what we do with it." The proposed refuge would preserve the habitats of hundreds of species of animals, including caribou, moose, musk oxen, wolves, polar and grizzly bears, and many kinds of birds.

After years of lobbying, the Muries got their wish in 1960, when the government set aside 8.9 million acres (about 9,000 square miles) in north-eastern Alaska as Arctic National Wildlife Refuge. This government designation ensured that the area would remain permanently free from development. Margaret recalled that when they heard the good news, "Olaus was at his table at the back of the room, writing. I held out the telegram to him; he read it and stood and took me in his arms and we both wept."

Following this triumph, the Muries spent a great deal of time campaigning on behalf of the Wilderness Act, which would make the preservation of wilderness a government policy. Unfortunately, Olaus would not see the successful outcome of this battle; he died of cancer on October 21, 1963. One tribute to his life and work called him "a man of the world terrestrial, authority on its animal life, interpreter of nature's art, student of her design, exponent of the wilderness in terms of the human spirit." Olaus shared his intense feelings about the natural world with many people through his writing, painting, and activism. "He cherished the hope that the young might still have opportunities for great adventure if only our society is wise enough to keep some of the great country in both Canada and Alaska empty of development and full of life," Margaret explained.

When the Wilderness Act passed in 1964, setting aside 9 million acres of wild lands for future generations, Margaret was invited to the White House to watch President Lyndon Johnson sign it. Though she was deeply saddened by her husband's death, she was determined to continue the work that they had begun together. "Whatever happens, it's more fun to be in the performance than to stand with your face to the wall," she noted.

MARGARET'S WORK CONTINUES

Over the next three decades, Margaret remained active in environmental causes. She was a paid staff member of the Wilderness Society for many years and also acted as the group's vice president. In 1968, she lobbied successfully for the creation of North Cascades National Park in Washington. Later that year, however, vast oil fields were discovered in northern Alaska at Prudhoe Bay—an inlet of the Arctic Ocean on the North Slope of the Brooks Range, where the Muries had studied caribou many years before. Margaret knew that oil drilling in the area would threaten her beloved Arctic National Wildlife Refuge, so she again turned her attention toward preserving Alaskan wilderness.

In the 1970s, the United States was facing an oil crisis. As the major oil-producing countries of the Middle East began increasing their prices rapidly, the U.S. government grew determined to exploit the oil reserves at Prudhoe Bay. In order to do this, they planned to build an 800-mile pipeline to transport the oil all the way across Alaska from Prudhoe Bay to Valdez, a southern port that provided access to the Pacific Ocean. Though Murie and other environmentalists fought against the proposed pipeline, worrying that it might result in oil spills that would harm wildlife, the government decided to go ahead with the plan in 1973. The one positive thing to come out of the Alaskan pipeline, according to Murie, was that it helped residents change their way of thinking about the state's natural resources. "They see now how the land can be taken over and changed, and they are beginning to be truly concerned over what could happen to the land, to the future, the way of life of their children and their children's children," she explained.

In 1975, Murie traveled to Alaska as a consultant to the National Park Service. She was hired to explore several different remote areas and recommend which ones most deserved to be protected by the government as wilderness. During her travels, Murie met with people from all walks of life to hear their views on the benefits of the various areas. When she completed her study, she recommended that all of the areas be saved. "If we saved every scrap of wilderness we have, it wouldn't be enough," she stated. Murie argued that preserving the remaining Alaskan wilderness was the only way for America to have a future. "Surely the United States of America is not so poor we cannot afford to have these places, not so rich that we can do without them," she said. "I have known Alaska all these years. All Alaska needs to do is be Alaska."

In 1980, President Jimmy Carter signed the Alaska Lands Act, which established or enlarged over 30 national parks and wildlife refuges and protected 24 rivers in Alaska. The act also expanded Arctic National Wildlife Refuge, nearly doubling its size to 19.8 million acres. Though Murie was thrilled with most aspects of the Alaska Lands Act, she was disappointed that it excluded a key parcel of land along the Arctic coastline from permanent protection. This 1.5 million-acre area, often called "America's Serengeti" because of its abundant wildlife, was the heart of the region's ecology. Though the coastal plain was protected temporarily, the door was left open for possible future oil drilling and other development. In 1987, the government completed a study of the potential environmental impacts of oil drilling in the area. The final report admitted that there would be major negative impacts on wildlife and habitat, but—due to political considerations and heavy lobbying by oil companies—still recommended full-scale development of the area. Murie joined activists from a number of environmental groups in vocal protest against opening this section of the Arctic National Wildlife refuge to harmful oil drilling. As of 1996 the area remained protected, but it still faced a significant threat that its status would be changed by Congress.

Now past the age of 90, Margaret Murie continues to write letters, host meetings of environmentalists, and speak with students about the importance of preserving Arctic National Wildlife Refuge and other wilderness areas around the country. "I've had enough experiences for 12 lifetimes. So I feel that the least I can do is to try to save what little we have left for the future. I know a lot of young people will appreciate this country, if given a chance. But they can't if the country isn't there. It all comes back to what things we think are important in life," she explained. "Every citizen has a responsibility toward this planet. I'm counting on the new generation coming up. I have to believe in their spirit as those who came before me believed in mine."

MARRIAGE AND FAMILY

Margaret and Olaus Murie were married on August 19, 1924, in the small village of Anvik, Alaska. Their wedding was supposed to have taken place the previous day, but Olaus returned late from an expedition tagging birds at the mouth of the Yukon River. The couple eventually had three children: Martin, Joanne, and Donald. Margaret continues to live in a comfortable cabin near Jackson Hole, Wyoming.

WRITINGS

BY MARGARET MURIE

Two in the Far North, 1962
Wapiti Wilderness, 1966 (with Olaus Murie)
Island Between, 1978

BY OLAUS MURIE

The Elk of North America, 1951
Field Guide to Animal Tracks, 1954
Wapiti Wilderness, 1966 (with Margaret Murie)
Journeys to the Far North, 1973

HONORS AND AWARDS

MARGARET MURIE

Distinguished Alumna Award (University of Alaska, Fairbanks): 1967
Audubon Medal (National Audubon Society): 1980
John Muir Award (Sierra Club): 1983
Robert Marshall Conservation Award (Wilderness Society): 1986

OLAUS MURIE

Aldo Leopold Memorial Award (Wildlife Society): 1953, for *The Elk of North America*
Conservation Award (American Forestry Association): 1954
Cornelius Amory Pugsley Bronze Medal (American Scenic and Historic Preservation Society): 1954
Audubon Medal (National Audubon Society): 1959
Izaak Walton League Honor Roll in Conservation: 1960
John Muir Award (Sierra Club): 1963

FURTHER READING

BOOKS

Bryant, Jennifer. *Margaret Murie: A Wilderness Life*, 1993 (juvenile)
Contemporary Authors, Vol. 110
Keene, Ann T. *Earthkeepers: Observers and Protectors of Nature*, 1994 (juvenile)
LaBastille, Anne. *Women and Wilderness*, 1980

Murie, Adolph. *A Naturalist in Alaska,* 1963
Murie, Margaret. *Two in the Far North,* 1962
Murie, Olaus. *Journeys to the Far North,* 1973
Wild, Peter. *Pioneer Conservationists of Western America,* 1979

PERIODICALS

Audubon, July-Aug. 1950, p.224; Nov.-Dec. 1963, p.359; May 1980, p.106
National Wildlife, Oct.-Nov. 1992, p.26
New York Times, Oct. 24, 1963, p.A33

ADDRESS

The Wilderness Society
900 17th Street NW
Washington, D.C. 20006

OBITUARY

Patsy Ruth Oliver   1935-1993
American Grassroots Activist in the
"Environmental Justice" Movement
Led Fight to Relocate Families Living on
Toxic Waste Dump in Texarkana, Texas

BIRTH

Patsy Ruth Oliver was born in 1935 in Texarkana, Texas, a former railroad town on the Texas-Arkansas border. She was
raised by her mother, Mattie Warren.

YOUTH AND EDUCATION

Oliver grew up during the time of segregation in the American South, when there were separate facilities — schools, restaurants, clubs, buses, etc. — for whites and blacks. Like many other Southern cities, Texarkana experienced problems with racism during these years. As an African-American, Oliver saw more than her share. In fact, she recalled that there was a public lynching in the town as late as 1941. In that incident, white members of the Ku Klux Klan broke into the town jail, dragged out a black man who had been accused of raping a white woman, and killed him by hanging him from a tree in the middle of town. Oliver often had to walk past that tree as a little girl. "It put fear in your heart. It put anger in your heart. It made you want to fight," she stated. "I felt like I was caged into a system that only worked for white people."

Oliver grew up poor, and she had to start working at an early age in order to help support her family. She took her first job, as a maid, at the age of 10. During this time, she was also attending public schools in Texarkana. Later, she was employed for several years as a nurse's aide.

CAREER HIGHLIGHTS

Oliver never planned to become an environmental activist. Instead, she got married quite young and started raising a family. Once she had children of her own, Oliver needed to earn money to support them, so she accepted a position on the assembly line at the Lone Star Army Munitions Plant. The pay was as high as an African-American woman could expect at that time, but the job itself was very dangerous because it required workers to handle detonators for army explosives. "I never knew if my kids were going to greet me as a corpse or as a person," Oliver admitted, "but I took that chance to keep my children fed." She had scars from the time a detonator blew up in her hands.

Oliver first showed her inclination toward activism during the civil rights movement of the 1960s, when she participated in several protests against segregation in Texarkana. For example, she joined a sit-in at the Woolworth's lunch counter, which had been designated "whites only," and ended up being pelted with rotten eggs. And she was actually shot at during an organized wade-in at a white swimming area on the town's lake.

Also during the 1960s, Oliver divorced her first husband and moved into a public housing project (a government-subsidized dwelling for low-income families) with her five children and her mother. Even though living conditions in the housing project were not too bad, Oliver dreamed of buying a home of her own in a nice neighborhood, with a backyard where her children could play and she could plant a garden. In order to save enough money to achieve her dream, Oliver worked as a waitress on weekends and cooked for white families in her spare time in addition to her job at the munitions plant.

In 1967, Oliver overheard some women on a bus talking about a new subdivision that was being built for middle-class black families. It was going to be named Carver Terrace, after George Washington Carver. In the days of segregation, when many African-Americans in Texarkana did not even have access to public utilities, the new development sounded like a great opportunity to Oliver. She immediately went to the construction site and gave the developer a small down payment, then returned home to tell her family that they were going to live in a brand new house. "We're getting out of here," she told them. "I'm not going to live in a ghetto no more."

CARVER TERRACE NEIGHBORHOOD

For the first few years, life was great for Oliver and her family in their modest, ranch-style brick house. They enjoyed backyard barbeques with their neighbors, the children played outdoors and swam in the nearby creek, and Oliver planted the garden she had always wanted. "Little did I know I was living on a time bomb," she stated later. "It was ticking, but we could not hear it. It was like a rattlesnake that has lost its rattles: it is still a rattlesnake, but it is even deadlier because you do not know it is there—and it may kill you before you even see it."

Gradually, many of the 250 residents of Carver Terrace—all of whom were African-Americans—began noticing strange and disturbing things about their neighborhood. For example, the tap water smelled like tar, and an oily black residue accumulated in sinks and tubs. Water pipes became corroded and burst frequently. Everyone in the area had trouble getting their lawns to grow and continually had to buy fresh topsoil. Something ate a hole through the bottom of children's plastic swimming pools if they sat outside for a few days. People's pets began to get sick and die.

Finally, the neighbors started comparing notes and realized that most of them had not been feeling well for quite some time. Nearly all the Carver Terrace families reported experiencing health problems like headaches, upset stomachs, dizzy spells, shortness of breath, and skin rashes. "At night you'd wake up with a headache," Oliver remembered of those early years. "It felt like a hangover, but you knew you didn't drink anything stronger than water. You'd come out of the shower and have a burning sensation. And when you toweled off, it felt like you were rubbing your flesh raw."

119

As time passed, many of the residents' minor ailments turned into more serious illnesses, such as cancer and liver, kidney, and heart disease. People in the neighborhood began making frequent trips to the hospital, and several died. "It got to the place where the hearse was out there more than the yellow cabs," Oliver noted. Oliver herself, who had always been very healthy, suffered from a tumor on her thyroid gland and a ruptured gallbladder. Her new husband, Nathaniel, had a painful cyst on his kidney.

Despite the suspicious nature of their health problems, the residents of Carver Terrace were reluctant to admit that their surroundings might be making them sick. "We were just thrilled to be able to buy such nice homes in Texarkana, a city long noted for its dismal race relations," Oliver recalled. "You just tried to place the blame everywhere but on your dream. I suppose when you're trying to be happy, when you're feeling successful for the first time, you don't want to ask questions. You don't really want to know."

TOXIC WASTE DUMP DISCOVERED

In 1979 — responding to the public outrage that resulted when deadly chemicals were found buried under the middle-class suburb of Love Canal, New York (see entry on Lois Gibbs in this volume of *Biography Today*) — the U.S. government required the nation's 50 largest chemical companies to identify the sites where they had contaminated the environment with toxic waste. One firm in the industry, the Koppers Company, noted that it had operated a wood-treatment plant in the area that later became the Carver Terrace neighborhood. The company admitted that during the 50 years that the plant was in operation, it had seriously polluted the area's soil and water.

The plant's main business had been coating wooden railroad ties with creosote — a toxic chemical made from coal tar. Koppers Company had not only allowed the chemical to drip on the ground, but had disposed of used creosote by dumping it into a huge "waste lagoon" on their property. When the plant was bulldozed in 1961 to make way for the Carver Terrace development, the creosote tanks were simply buried and the homes were built on the contaminated soil. "Deadly poisons lay in the soil beneath our homes, and when the temperature and weather were right, those poisons rose into the air for us to breathe, and rainfall moved the poisons around," Oliver stated. Scientists now know that exposure to creosote can cause all the health problems that the residents experienced, including cancer.

In 1980, the Texas Department of Water Resources sent investigators to the Carver Terrace neighborhood to find out the extent of the problem. In addition to creosote, they discovered dangerous levels of arsenic, pentachlorophenol (PCP), and polyaromatic hydrocarbons. All of these chemicals, which are known carcinogens (cancer-causing agents), were contaminating the residents' soil and groundwater. Despite the obvious risks to people's health, however, the investigators did not release their findings. "The first inkling residents had that they were living on a time bomb came then—but not in any official communication. During the field investigation, some of the investigators gave informal warnings to some residents, telling them that they should be careful about their children playing outdoors," Oliver recalled. "But officially, residents were told nothing of the hazards of living in Carver Terrace."

In October 1984, the 62-acre former site of the Koppers plant was added to the Superfund National Priority List. The Environmental Protection Agency (EPA) began compiling the list in 1980, in an effort to identify and clean up the nation's worst toxic waste dumps. The government originally allocated $1.6 billion for the clean-up efforts and expected to collect much more from the companies that had caused the pollution. The Superfund program became increasingly controversial over the years, however, as its budget ballooned to 10 times the original amount. Because it was often difficult to get polluters to pay for their past actions, the EPA seemed to spend more time and money on finding polluters and taking them to court than on cleaning up sites and helping people whose lives were affected.

After Carver Terrace was designated as a Superfund site, the EPA sent crews to conduct an extensive study of the area and decide on the best approach for cleaning it up. During meetings with the residents at this time, representatives of the government agency admitted that the neighborhood contained toxic chemicals but insisted that there was no immediate danger to people's health. Whenever EPA investigators came to sample the soil or water, however, they were covered from head to toe in "moon suits" and gas masks designed to protect them from exposure to hazardous substances. Residents questioned why such precautions were necessary if the area really was safe, but they never received a satisfactory answer.

As the EPA study dragged on, the people of Carver Terrace found more and more reasons to be worried about their environment. One time, for example, Oliver sat on her porch and watched an EPA employee struggling to complete a field study in the Texas summer heat. In a neighborly gesture, she went into her house, poured some 7-Up into a glass, and came out to offer it to him. Assuming that the clear liquid was tap water, the employee became very flustered, emphatically claimed that he was not thirsty, and refused to drink it. "You would've thought I'd pulled a .38 magnum on him," Oliver said of his reaction. And all this time the EPA had been telling the residents that the water was safe to drink.

121

The EPA's preliminary investigation ended up taking eight years. During this time, the main action the government took was to close a gravel pit near the Carver Terrace neighborhood, putting a chain-link fence around it and posting a sign that read, "Soil contaminated with toxic waste. Keep out." This seemed ridiculous to many of the residents. "Our toxics down here are real intelligent," Oliver said sarcastically. "They can read. They'll stay on that side of the fence." In the meantime, as they continued to experience health problems and struggled to pay their medical bills, 64 families filed suit against Koppers Company for damages caused by the pollution. When the case came to trial, however, a predominantly white jury refused to award the residents any money, saying that they had failed to prove that their illnesses were caused by exposure to the chemicals. The race of the jury members may have been important, because Oliver and others later came to believe that racism was a key factor in their struggle.

When the EPA finally released its report in 1988, it was four volumes long and took two people to carry. It detailed an $8 million clean-up plan that would involve replacing all the topsoil in the area with clean dirt. The report claimed that this plan would take care of the problem and allow residents to remain in the neighborhood with minimal risks to their health. But Oliver and her neighbors did not believe a word of it. During the whole eight-year study, EPA investigators had never interviewed any of the people living in the area, so the residents felt that the report dismissed many legitimate causes of concern. For example, the report admitted that nearby Wagner Creek was heavily contaminated, but noted that it was "hard to imagine" anyone swimming in its muddy waters. In fact, all the neighborhood children had done so regularly. The report also stated that eating vegetables grown in the toxic soil could prove hazardous, but investigators claimed that they had not observed any vegetable gardens. In actuality, many of the neighbors had gardens; the Olivers grew and ate their own vegetables all the time.

Feeling disappointed, angry, and betrayed by the EPA's conclusions — as well as by the fact that no one had warned them of the dangers they had faced for all those years — some of the residents began to do their own investigative work. They soon found two additional government studies warning of the health risks posed by toxic chemicals in the Carver Terrace neighborhood. One of these studies, which by law should have been made available to the residents, openly accused the EPA of underestimating the risks.

FIGHT FOR RELOCATION

Oliver and the other residents no longer trusted the government to do what was in their best interest. They were stirred to action by their anger about how they had been treated. Oliver decided that her top priority was getting her family and her neighbors out of the area as soon as possible. She began insisting that the government purchase all 79 homes in the neighborhood and help the families relocate to safer areas. Although similar buyout and relocation programs had been enacted for the residents of Love Canal and several other communities endangered by toxic waste, the suggestion met with strong resistance from the EPA. At this time, Oliver began to suspect that racism was behind the government's attitude. "If there's one thing I know, it's racism," she stated.

In order to increase the pressure on the EPA to meet her demands, Oliver joined an environmental group known as Friends United for a Safe Environment (FUSE), organized petition drives and protest marches, and traveled by bus to visit elected officials in the state capital in Austin and in Washington, D.C. Oliver recalled that she sometimes surprised herself with her passionate involvement in the Carver Terrace relocation campaign. "I didn't know beans about toxics. I was a nurse and a housewife and a mother. What did I know? But suddenly, everything I had worked for in my life was up for grabs—because of toxics. My American dream had turned into an American nightmare," she stated. "I could have been one of the people hiding behind their curtains and watching the march go by. But here I was leading the damn thing!"

As she worked to raise public awareness of her cause, Oliver met and enlisted the support of several prominent African-American leaders, including Benjamin Chavis, who later became director of the National Association for the Advancement of Colored People (NAACP), and the Reverend Jesse Jackson. She also arranged to be interviewed frequently on the local television news, and she even appeared in a video sponsored by the environmental group Greenpeace that appeared on the cable music channel VH-1. "We had to inform the general public about our plight if we were ever going to win," Oliver explained. "We knew we could not leave it up to the EPA or the state of Texas." In February 1989, Oliver and her neighbors hosted the Conference on Environmental Justice, a national meeting of environmentalists. "Environmentalists from all over the country swarmed into Carver Terrace and saw what we were up against," Oliver recalled. "This was a landmark event for Carver Terrace and probably did more to help us eventually get out of our nightmare than the years of administrative foot-dragging of the EPA."

In November 1990, under tremendous pressure from environmental organizations and Texas constituents who had heard about the plight of Carver Terrace, Congressman Jim Chapman sponsored federal legislation that overrode the EPA's recommendations and allocated $5 million to relocate Oliver and the other residents of the poisoned neighborhood. While they were thrilled to have finally won their fight, the residents were disappointed that the government did not take any steps to recognize or compensate them for the health problems that continued to plague them. It was a particularly bittersweet victory for Oliver, whose mother had died of cancer earlier that year. Adding to their disappointment, the residents learned that the U.S. Army Corps of Engineers had to survey and assign a value to their property before the buyout and relocation could occur. This process ended up taking another three years, during which time the Carver Terrace families continued to be exposed to dangerous chemicals.

Oliver finally received her settlement and moved to a new northeast Texas home in June 1993, after living on one of the country's worst toxic waste dumps for 25 years. As the residents were relocated, Carver Terrace turned into a boarded-up ghost town. A journalist visiting the site afterward reported smelling the odor of hot tar in the air, seeing large patches of creosote-soaked dead grass around houses and under swing sets, and watching toxic muck ooze to the surface of a small hole in the ground. The remains of the neighborhood were demolished in 1994, and the EPA set up facilities to begin cleaning the soil and the groundwater. The clean-up process was still going on as of 1996, and the former residents had yet to recover any of their medical expenses.

ENVIRONMENTAL JUSTICE MOVEMENT

The plight of Oliver's Carver Terrace neighborhood, which has sometimes been called "the black Love Canal," became a rallying cry for the "environmental justice" movement. The movement grew out of a 1987 report by the United Church of Christ's Commission for Racial Justice. This report found that communities populated by minorities were far more likely than those populated by whites to be affected by the dumping of toxic waste. In fact, the report claimed that three out of every five people of color in the United States lived in areas that were at risk from pollution. A later study found that it took the government significantly longer both to identify and clean up toxic waste dumps in minority neighborhoods.

Some activists call this phenomenon "environmental racism," and believe that industries and municipalities intentionally pollute minority areas because they think the residents lack the political power to fight back. Oliver seemed to agree with this assessment of the situation. When she chose a new neighborhood to live in, she made sure that it was integrated. "I don't care if it's chocolate swirl or chocolate chip, but you won't see me in an all-black neighborhood anymore," she stated. "I don't ever want to be that powerless again. The next time I get rained on, I want white people around me. Whatever's going to kill me is going to kill them, too."

Following the death of her mother, Oliver dedicated the rest of her life to the cause of environmental justice. "I am an environmentalist. I always will be, so long as God gives me breath," she explained. "I have been fortunate to meet environmental activists in the movement who are dedicated to the cause of justice." She was actively involved with several environmental and social organizations, serving on the boards of Friends of the Earth and the National Toxics Campaign, and on the coordinating committee of the Southwest Network for Economic and Environmental Justice. She also spent a great deal of time helping people in other areas fight their own environmental battles. "Patsy typifies what's happening in the environmental justice movement in communities of color," sociologist Robert Bullard commented. "It's mostly women who get involved to protect family, home, and community. These are not traditional environmentalists. These are people talking about survival."

Sadly, Oliver's career as an environmental activist was cut short when she died suddenly of a heart attack near the end of 1993. Before she died, Oliver offered the following advice to young activists: "Join hands with other environmentalists, social justice activists, and concerned citizens far and wide. Make contact with the national environmental groups that have expertise you feel will be useful to your struggle. . . . At the same time, *always* help other grassroots environmental organizations. You will need to keep building the network. Somebody else's cause that you help will be your own—because we all live downstream from someone. You may make mistakes; we did. But you will learn from them. Keep growing and learning. Never say die, and keep on, even when winning your fight looks like an impossible dream. We learned in Carver Terrace that even an impossible dream, like getting out of our prison of poison, can become a reality."

MARRIAGE AND FAMILY

Oliver's first marriage—to a career military man—ended in the early 1960s, after they had five children together. She married Nathaniel Oliver, a seaman and cook, in 1979. One of her children, Stephanie, died of a stroke in October 1993, shortly before Oliver's own death. Tragically, Oliver was only able to enjoy living in her new northeast Texas home, which she had fought so long to obtain, for six months before she died.

WRITINGS

"Living on a Superfund Site in Texarkana," in *Unequal Protection: Environmental Justice and Communities of Color* (edited by Robert D. Bullard), 1994

OLIVER'S PHILOSOPHY

"So many people don't think one person can make a difference, and really it has to start some place. So, let it start with me."

FURTHER READING

BOOKS

Bullard, Robert D., ed. *Unequal Protection: Environmental Justice and Communities of Color*, 1994
Kozol, Jonathan. *Savage Inequalities*, 1991

PERIODICALS

Friends of the Earth, Jan. 1994, p.11
The Humanist, Nov.-Dec. 1994, p.45
Vogue, Nov. 1993, p.214

OBITUARY

Roger Tory Peterson 1908-1996
American Conservationist and Bird Expert
Author of *A Field Guide to the Birds* and
Other Nature Guides

BIRTH

Roger Tory Peterson was born on August 28, 1908, in
Jamestown, New York. His father, Charles Gustav Peterson,
worked in a local furniture factory, while his mother,
Henrietta Bader Peterson, took care of Roger, his sister
Margaret, and their sickly grandmother.

YOUTH

Peterson's parents found that their only son was a bright but aggravating boy. A very intelligent child, Peterson had moved on to high school by the time he was 12 years old. But he was headstrong and mischievous, too, and he got in more than his share of trouble. Looking back on his youth, Peterson himself admitted that "I might even have wound up in a reform school if I had not developed my interest in birds." As he grew older, his interest in the outdoors limited the amount of mischief that he got into in his neighborhood, but his parents never knew when he might run off unannounced to explore in the woods. He was fascinated by all aspects of nature, from birds to flowers to insects, and even when his parents managed to keep him at home, he could usually be found reading books about nature.

Both Peterson's father, who was a stern disciplinarian, and the other boys of the neighborhood were baffled by the youngster's passion for nature. Charles Peterson admitted that his son knew a lot about animals, and especially birds, but he thought that the knowledge would not be useful to him when he was older. Meanwhile, Peterson's classmates—who were older than him since he had skipped a couple of grades—were not sure what to make of the skinny boy. "Mostly," wrote John C. Devlin and Grace Naismith in *The World of Roger Tory Peterson*, "they were puzzled by him and amused at this 'strangest boy in town,' who sometimes arrived in school with such things as snakes, toads, or bird eggs in his pockets, sometimes smelling like a skunk after catching one in a butterfly net."

As he grew older, Peterson proved adept at removing obstacles that would have prevented a less imaginative boy from indulging his enjoyment of the outdoors. One day, for instance, Peterson decided that the town's curfew law—which called for all children to be off the streets fairly early in the evening—was hindering his efforts to catch moths for his insect collection. The moths he wanted did not appear around the city's streetlights until well after the beginning of the curfew. Typically, he decided to confront the problem head-on. "I trotted down to the City Hall and explained my problem to the police chief," he later recalled. "His action was decisive. Turning to his secretary, he instructed her to type out a permit which read simply: 'This permits Roger Peterson to catch moths around streetlights until 11 p.m. Signed, F. Johnson, Chief of Police.' That piece of paper gave me a real status—a lot of status for a boy of 12."

EDUCATION

Peterson was a good student, although his opinionated nature sometimes got him in trouble with his teachers. He recalled that his relationship with his high-school biology teacher was particularly poor. "I would take issue with her from time to time. She didn't like that. She made the statement that the snowy egret was extinct and I had to correct her. What she said had been nearly true 20 years earlier but circumstances had changed and the snowy egret had made a comeback. I had no compunctions about bringing up such points in class. So my biology marks were not very good. I was a bit of a free spirit when it came time to expressing my own views."

Peterson enjoyed many aspects of high school, though. He was a good student in both mechanical drawing and writing, two subjects that would help him greatly in his later years. He also took advantage of the school system's extracurricular clubs. Peterson joined both the Junior Audubon Society and the Bird and Tree Club at school, and he was an enthusiastic member of both outdoor organizations. When he was not watching or studying birds, he could often be found painting portraits of owls, cardinals, sparrows, and other birds that caught his fancy.

In 1925 Peterson graduated from Jamestown High School. After graduating he worked during the day as a painter, but in the evening he devoted his energies to his real passion: birds. By this time he was a dedicated birdwatcher, and his paintings of birds during this time reflected his encyclopedic knowledge of their appearance and characteristics. A few of his paintings even appeared in bird art exhibitions, and a number of people urged him to go to an art school so that he could further develop his talent.

Heeding their advice, Peterson moved to New York, where he studied at the Art Students League from 1927 to 1928, and at the National Academy of Design from 1929 to 1931. He also became heavily involved in the activities of a couple of area nature clubs. The most important of these clubs was the Bronx County Bird Club, an active and knowledgeable group of birdwatching enthusiasts. Peterson later said that if he had not joined the club "I would have devoted my life to painting. Birding would have been a hobby."

CAREER HIGHLIGHTS

After concluding his course work at the National Academy of Design in 1931, Peterson spent the summer as a camp counselor at Camp Chewonki, located on the coast of Maine. He made valuable contacts at the camp, to which he returned for the next four summers. One of these contacts, Clarence Allen, convinced Peterson to join him as an assistant at Rivers Country Day School, a prosperous prep school in the Boston area. Peterson spent the next three years living in the Boston area.

DEVELOPMENT OF *A FIELD GUIDE TO THE BIRDS*

By the early 1930s all of Peterson's friends recognized that he was an amazingly knowledgeable authority on birds. While out walking with

Peterson one day, one of them, author William Vogt, encouraged him to put together a guidebook that would help other birdwatchers. Vogt recalled that "Roger possessed a prodigious keenness of sight and hearing, and on this particular December morning I was again impressed by his expertness. . . . 'Roger,' I said to him, 'you know more about identifying the birds of this region than almost anyone else, and you can paint. Why don't you pass on your knowledge to other people in a book?'" Peterson was intrigued by the idea, in part because he had such a low opinion of other bird guides that were already out on the market. After Vogt assured him that he would help him find a publisher for the book, Peterson began work on the project.

As Peterson worked on the book, he arranged its contents so that it would be easy for its users to consult. "I grouped birds that look alike and therefore might be mistaken for each other, instead of grouping them by species," he remembered. "I made my paintings schematic and two-dimensional, and I drew little arrows to point out the 'field marks' that are the main information you need to identify a bird. Those arrows were my invention." Peterson also arranged for the book to be published in a smaller size so that it would be easier for birdwatchers to take out into the field. Finally, instead of using big words and scientific terminology that often confused users of other guides, Peterson provided clear, accurate descriptions of the birds and their distinguishing marks. These innovations, he felt, would make his book much easier to use than other guides that had been published in the past.

A FIELD GUIDE TO THE BIRDS

Published in 1934, *A Field Guide to Birds* was an immediate success. Its initial print run of 2,000 copies sold out in a week, and the surprised publisher scrambled to print more copies (more than two million copies of the book have been sold over the years). Peterson was amazed at the book's popularity, which was aided by positive reviews. After the success of this first book, which only discussed birds in the East, he began to make plans for a second book that would cover birds in the Western United States.

Looking back on his first book, Peterson was very critical of it: "I shudder every time I look at it. The drawings are horrible. I revised it completely in 1939 and spent a full year revising it again after the war, but I am still not satisfied." Critics and members of the conservation community, though, have an entirely different view of the book's merits. They point out that the success of the first book spawned a whole series of Peterson's guides, and that these books triggered an explosion in the popularity of birdwatching (*National Geographic* writer Douglas Chadwick estimated that by 1996 birdwatching was adding between five and nine billion dollars to the U.S. economy every year). As more people were drawn to birdwatching (or birding, as it is sometimes called), interest in nature and conservation increased as well. "Roger Tory Peterson," wrote Frank Graham Jr., "exerted an enormous influence on natural history and conservation" through his nature guides. "Rachel Carson's *Silent Spring* may have jolted Americans into the Age of Ecology in the 1960s, but they had been prepared for the transition by a succession of Peterson field guides over the previous three decades."

In the fall of 1934 Peterson accepted an editorial position with the National Association of Audubon Societies. This move marked the beginning of a long and fruitful association with the organization. A year later he was appointed education director for the society and named art director of the organization's magazine, *Bird Lore* (later known as *Audubon*).

Within a year or two of joining Audubon, Peterson had become quite well known in America's conservationist community. After all, his *Field Guide to the Birds* was still selling briskly, and many people had begun citing the book as a major factor in increasing public interest in the natural world. "Recognition is the first step toward preservation," Peterson was fond of saying. "Every birder becomes to some degree an ecologist. In political terms he is a conservationist." The author's name became so well known that even the Boy Scouts approached him in the hope that he would help the group update the birdwatching section of its manual. Peterson gladly complied.

MILITARY SERVICE

In 1943—two years after he published his second book, *A Field Guide to Western Birds*—Peterson was drafted into the U.S. Army to help battle Germany in World War II. "At the induction center I listed myself as an artist. I should have called myself a biologist, but my academic training had been basically as an artist, and there was always camouflage [work]," he said.

Peterson's background did indeed prove useful to the army's camouflage program, which was concerned with devising designs that would help hide American soldiers and vehicles from the enemy. But he also contributed to the American war effort in some unusual ways. Since Peterson was an accomplished writer and illustrator, he produced instruction manuals for such diverse operations as road building and bomb defusing. In addition, the army developed a plane spotting and identification technique that was based in large part on the bird expert's own method of bird identification.

Despite his responsibilities in the armed forces, Peterson still found time to pursue his interest in birding. He often spent his free time exploring nearby forests with a sketchpad, notebook, or camera. On one memorable occasion, his interest in birds triggered a change in the base's training operations. Peterson, who was a private at the time, discovered that a horned lark had built a nest on the parade ground of the base he was stationed at. "Under ordinary circumstances, I'd go through sergeants and up to the captain" to try and get the parade route altered, he said. "But these particular sergeants had absolutely no sympathy with something like a lark's nest on the parade ground." Peterson was determined to save the nest, though, so he showed it to the 11-year-old daughter of a colonel at the base. A short time later, after his bird-loving daughter returned from her walk, the colonel announced that the line of the parade should be rerouted away from the lark's nest. Even many years later, Peterson recalled that clever maneuver with great satisfaction.

During Peterson's last months in the military, he helped do research on the chemical DDT, a pesticide that some people thought could be used to eradicate mosquito populations on Pacific islands. Other military officers, though, wondered whether the chemical was safe, so a period of testing was arranged. Peterson was responsible for studying the impact of DDT

on bird populations. "At the time," he said, "we had no idea about the residual effects [of DDT] and that birds that were in long food chains, such as pelicans, peregrines, etc., would be so adversely affected. Our work was a beginning of some of the research which Rachel Carson so intelligently interpreted later" (see entry on Rachel Carson in this volume of *Biography Today*).

PETERSON'S REPUTATION GROWS

After completing his World War II military service, Peterson returned to writing, painting, and photography. He reached an agreement with Houghton Mifflin, the company that had published his first two books, to edit a whole series of nature books, and he busied himself with an ambitious schedule of other writing and painting projects as well. Observers might have expected Peterson's pace to ease somewhat as the years passed, but he remained a remarkably prolific artist for the next half-century. In addition to the many books that he wrote, edited, or illustrated, he contributed numerous articles to various magazines, wrote dozens of introductions to others' books, and supervised production of a number of nature films.

Peterson also emerged as an increasingly important member of the conservation movement by the latter part of the 1940s and the 1950s. In 1946 Peterson was named art director of the National Wildlife Federation, a position he held into the mid-1970s. In 1952 he was named to a two-year term as president of the American Nature Study Society, and a decade later he served the Wilson Ornithological Society as its president from 1964 to 1965. He also served long stints on the boards of directors of such organizations as the World Wildlife Fund and the Hawk Mountain Sanctuary Association. But Peterson remained most closely associated with the National Audubon Society, the organization with which he had first been linked. The author and painter served three different terms on the society's board of directors, and remained a special consultant to the group from 1970 to 1996, when he died.

PETERSON'S ENVIRONMENTAL VIEWS

By the time of Peterson's death on July 28, 1996, he was widely recognized as one of the most important conservationists of the twentieth century in America. People who had known him knew that he was not perfect—he had a bad temper, and many people thought that he became somewhat arrogant as his fame grew—but even his critics recognized that he was an important figure in developing America's environmental consciousness.

An aggressive and articulate spokesman on behalf of nature throughout his life, Peterson stressed that people needed to look beyond their own experiences and their own life spans to fully appreciate the complex nature of the planet and its inhabitants. "Most people still fail to appreciate the real meaning of extinction," he once said. "Extinction is not simply the vanishing of the whooping crane. It is not the vanishing of the Andean flamingo, nor the vanishing of the vicuna (a relative of the llama). It is the termination, the abrupt termination, of a long line of evolution."

Peterson also insisted that humankind needed to recognize the power that it had to shape the world, in both good and bad ways. "We, alone of all creatures, have it within our power to ravage the world or make it a garden. Men have already rendered uninhabitable large areas of the world, but they have restored others. Inevitably, observing cause and effect, I have become a conservationist. My fervent desire is to see the soils safeguarded, the waters unpolluted, the forests and grass lands properly managed and wildlife protected. To attain these ends means not only self-preservation but also a better future for the race. Conservation is plainly a moral issue."

MARRIAGE AND FAMILY

Peterson was married three times. He married his first wife, Mildred Washington, on December 19, 1936. The marriage lasted for a little more than seven years, during which they had three children. A short time after they divorced, on July 29, 1943, Peterson married Barbara Coulter, with whom he had two children, Tory and Lee. After a 32-year marriage, the couple divorced in March 1976. A month later, Peterson married Virginia Quinlan Westervelt, who survives him.

SELECTED WRITINGS

A Field Guide to the Birds, 1934
The Junior Book of Birds, 1939
A Field Guide to Western Birds, 1941
The Audubon Guide to Attracting Birds, 1941 (with John H. Baker)
Birds Over America, 1948
How to Know the Birds, 1949
Wildlife in Color, 1951
A Field Guide to the Birds of Britain and Europe, 1954 (with Guy Mountfort and P.A.D. Hollom)
Wild America, 1955 (with James Fisher)
The Bird Watcher's Anthology, 1957
A Field Guide to the Birds of Texas and Adjacent States, 1960
The Birds, 1963 (with the editors of *Life*)
The World of Birds, 1964 (with James Fisher)
A Field Guide to Wildflowers, 1968
A Field Guide to Mexican Birds, 1973 (with Edward L. Chalif)
Peterson First Guide to Birds, 1986
Peterson First Guide to Wildflowers, 1986
Save the Birds, 1989
The Field Guide Art of Roger Tory Peterson, 1990
Roger Tory Peterson's ABC of Birds: A Book for Little Birdwatchers, 1995

HONORS AND AWARDS

William Brewster Award (American Ornithologists' Union): 1944
John Burroughs Medal (John Burroughs Memorial Association): 1950
Geoffrey St. Hilaire Gold Medal (French Natural History Society): 1958
Conservation Award (White Memorial Foundation): 1968
Gold Medal (African Safari Club of Philadelphia): 1968
Paul Bartsch Award (Audubon Naturalist Society): 1969
Frances K. Hutchinson Medal (Garden Club of America): 1970
Audubon Medal (National Audubon Society): 1971
Gold Medal (World Wildlife Fund): 1972
Joseph Wood Krutch Medal (Humane Society of the United States): 1973
Oak Leaf Cluster Award (Audubon Naturalist Society): 1974
Explorers Medal (Explorers Club): 1974
Conservation Achievement Award (National Wildlife Federation): 1975

Cosmos Club Award: 1976
Green World Award (New York Botanical Garden): 1976
Linnaeus Gold Medal (Swedish Academy of Sciences): 1976
Horatio Alger Award: 1977
Master Bird Artist Medal (Leigh Yankee Museum): 1978
Ludlow Griscom Award (American Birding Association): 1980
Smithsonian Medal (Smithsonian Institution): 1984
Award of Merit (Chicago Field Museum of Natural History): 1986
Silver Buffalo Award (Boy Scouts of America): 1986

FURTHER READING

BOOKS

Benet's Reader's Encyclopedia of American Literature, 1991
Contemporary Authors, New Revision Series, Vol. 1
Devlin, John C., and Grace Naismith. *The World of Roger Tory Peterson,* 1977
Encyclopedia Britannica, 1985
Roger Tory Peterson: The Art and Photography of the World's Foremost Birder,
    1995 (co-edited by Rudy Hoglund, text by William Zinsser)
Peterson, Roger Tory. *A Field Guide to Birds,* 1934
Who's Who in America, 1996

PERIODICALS

American Heritage, Dec. 1996, p.18
Audubon, Sep./Oct. 1996, p.120
Boys' Life, June 1994, p.30
National Geographic, Oct. 1996, p.2
National Wildlife, Oct.-Nov. 1996, p.62
New York State Conservationist, Dec. 1995, p.19
New York Times, July 30, 1996, p.A1
New York Times Book Review, Aug. 13, 1995, p.16
Newsweek, Aug. 12, 1996, p.60
Time, Aug. 12, 1996, p.67

WORLD WIDE WEB SITES

http://www.rtpi.org
http://www.petersononline.com

OBITUARY

Ken Saro-Wiwa   1941-1995
Nigerian Author and Environmental/
Human Rights Activist
Protested Exploitation of Ogoni Lands by
Shell and Other Multinational Oil Companies
Executed by Nigeria's Military Government
despite Worldwide Pleas for Clemency

BIRTH

Kenule Beeson Saro-Wiwa was born on October 10, 1941, in
Bori, Rivers State, Nigeria. His father was a tribal chief among

the Ogoni people, so Saro-Wiwa was raised in a comfortable home along with many brothers and sisters.

A BRIEF HISTORY OF NIGERIA

Nigeria was undergoing major changes during Saro-Wiwa's youth. As the country gained its independence from Great Britain in the late 1950s, it seemed likely to become one of the leading nations in Africa. At that time, Nigeria had a democratic government, an educated population, and relatively peaceful relations among its three major ethnic groups and 250 smaller ones. It also had abundant farmland and rich underground oil reserves. The government implemented a plan of exporting food and oil in order to make money to build roads, schools, and hospitals and improve the quality of life enjoyed by the Nigerian people.

In 1966, however, the Hausa-Fulani tribe from northern Nigeria took control of the government and installed a military dictatorship. Before long, people of the Biafran region in southern Nigeria—which includes Saro-Wiwa's home, Ogoniland—revolted against the new regime. After a bloody conflict that lasted several years, the rebellion was finally crushed in 1970. During this time, thousands of tribespeople in Biafra died of starvation. The Hausa-Fulani leaders then claimed that all the land in southern Nigeria belonged to the government and signed a contract granting rights to the huge, multinational oil company Royal Dutch Shell to develop oil production facilities throughout the region.

As the Nigerian government quickly became dependent on oil for the majority of its revenues (82 percent by 1974, compared to 26 percent in 1970), it also became increasingly repressive and corrupt. Easy oil money transformed Nigerian politics until the nation was ruled by greed, with officials routinely receiving bribes and kickbacks. The country's elite leaders built luxurious homes inside guarded compounds and bought expensive cars, while the majority of the population struggled in conditions of unemployment and poverty. The annual income of an average Nigerian dropped consistently—from $1,200 in 1978 to $300 by the 1990s—and most villages still have no electricity, running water, paved roads, or hospitals. "Crude oil, once viewed as the means of Nigeria's ascent to greatness, had instead greased the skids into chaos," Joshua Hammer wrote in *Harper's* in 1996.

YOUTH

As conditions grew worse for the people of Nigeria, Saro-Wiwa felt increasingly resentful toward the government and the oil companies. Even as a young man, he was determined someday to lead his people in protest and force the situation to change. "He wanted to create a campaign modeled after the American civil rights movement," one friend recalled, "with mass protests, sit-ins, boycotts, vigils."

EDUCATION

Saro-Wiwa received his early education in schools run by missionaries (people who hoped to convert Africans to Christianity), then went on to high school in Umuahia, a village in southeastern Nigeria. His grades in high school were good enough to earn him a scholarship to attend the University of Ibadan, which was the premier college in Nigeria. During his college years, Saro-Wiwa excelled in writing and acted as the editor of several magazines, including *Mellanbite, Horizon,* and *Umuahia Times.* He graduated from the university in 1965, earning his bachelor of arts degree with honors.

CAREER HIGHLIGHTS

Immediately after graduating from college, Saro-Wiwa worked as a teacher—first at his old high school, and later at universities in Lagos and eastern Nigeria. He got fired in 1973, however, after he began to express his increasingly militant views on Nigerian politics and Ogoni rights. He held various jobs after he left teaching; for several years, he owned and operated a grocery store.

Saro-Wiwa's writing career started in the early 1970s, when a few of his radio plays were produced by the British Broadcasting Corporation (BBC). He did not really gain a reputation as a writer until 1985, though, when he published *Sozaboy: A Novel in Rotten English.* The story of a young man fighting in the rebel army during the Biafran conflict, this antiwar novel attracted critical praise both in Africa and abroad. Saro-Wiwa continued to publish short stories, poems, essays, and plays through the early 1990s, when he quit writing to become a full-time political and environmental activist.

Over the course of his career, Saro-Wiwa used his writing to draw attention to Nigeria's problems in a darkly funny way. For example, he wrote and produced one of the most popular television shows in Nigeria, "Basi and Company," beginning in 1989. This situation comedy poking fun at the country's "get-rich-quick" attitude was watched by 30 million Nigerians each week. "I believe in using satire as my weapon to fight," Saro-Wiwa explained. "The satirist holds up a distorting mirror before the people who get scared when they see their reflection. There are many scared people in Nigeria."

PLIGHT OF THE OGONI

Though Saro-Wiwa felt angry about the overall political situation in Nigeria—especially the greedy attitudes of the Nigerian government and Shell Oil—he was particularly concerned with the impact it had on his own Ogoni people. Ogoniland occupies 400 square miles on the Niger Delta in southeastern Nigeria. Though the area is rich with oil and natural gas deposits, the Ogoni people traditionally made their living by farming the fertile soil and fishing. Shell began oil-drilling operations there in 1958 and soon found it to be very profitable. The type of oil found under the ground in Ogoniland is easily refined into gasoline, and—unlike its operations in most other parts of the world—the company did not have to cope with any costly environmental regulations there.

Since their land was technically owned by the military government, the Ogoni people did not have the power to negotiate with Shell for a portion of the profits or to complain when the oil operations polluted the environment. As a result, Ogoniland suffered the consequences of massive oil production activities without gaining any of the financial benefits. During the years that Shell operated in Ogoniland, oil spills destroyed thousands of acres of farmland and fouled fishing streams and drinking water supplies. "Oil spills are very common," noted one villager. "The oil just sits there. It is not cleaned up. For one spill, Shell hired a contractor who just burned it off." In fact, there were 111 major oil spills between 1985 and 1994 alone, and puddles of oil as large as football fields dotted the land.

Shell claimed to abide by the same environmental standards in Nigeria that it used elsewhere. Yet the company burned off a huge amount of natural gas at its oil wells there—76 percent, compared to 0.6 percent that is burned off in the United States. The burning of natural gas releases harmful chemicals that contribute to global warming. In Ogoniland, constant gas flares covered the surrounding towns with greasy, toxic soot. "This action has destroyed wildlife and plant life, and has made the residents half-deaf and prone to respiratory diseases," Saro-Wiwa wrote. "Whenever it rains in Ogoni, all we have is acid rain which further poisons watercourses, streams, creeks, and agricultural land."

Though wells in Ogoniland have produced $30 billion in oil over nearly 40 years, the Ogoni—prevented from enjoying their traditional way of life— have become desperately poor. At one point the Nigerian government agreed to return 3 percent of the annual oil revenues to the people of the region, but nearly all of the money disappeared into the pockets of corrupt officials before it could do any good. Due to the lack of schools and hospitals, Ogoniland now has a 20 percent literacy rate and one of the highest infant-mortality rates in the country. "Oil exploration has turned Ogoni into a wasteland," Saro-Wiwa stated. "In return we have received nothing . . . the interest of the few like the Ogonis was bound to suffer." Gradually, the Ogoni people began to rise up in scattered protests against Shell and the military government.

FORMATION OF MOSOP

For Saro-Wiwa, the last straw in the exploitation of the Ogoni and their land took place in October 1990. At that time, people from the Ogoni village of Umuechem organized a peaceful protest against the pollution of their lands by oil spills. They occupied part of a Shell oil refinery to call attention to their plight and demanded compensation for lost farmlands. Shell officials, wanting to discourage future protests, asked for help from the Nigerian Mobile Police Force. The next day, the police stormed into the village, killing 80 people and destroying nearly 500 homes, in order to teach the protesters a lesson.

Horrified by these events, Saro-Wiwa and other members of Ogoniland's educated elite formed the Movement for the Survival of Ogoni People (MOSOP) to better organize resistance. The group's first action was to draft a 10-point Ogoni Bill of Rights, in which they demanded $10 billion in reparations from Shell and a degree of political autonomy from the government. "If nothing is done now, the Ogoni people will be extinct within 10 years," Saro-Wiwa wrote at the time. "This matter is urgent. I live in the hope that somewhere in this world, good still exists and that it will prevail over evil."

By 1993, more than half the population of Ogoniland — or about 300,000 people — had pledged their support to MOSOP and its principles. Thanks to the international standing he had gained through his writing, Saro-Wiwa became the most prominent spokesman for MOSOP. People gathered from miles around to hear his eloquent and inspiring speeches. That January, he led his huge following on a peaceful protest march through Ogoniland. Around the same time, however, a radical youth wing of the organization began resorting to violence and sabotage to draw attention to their cause. Fearing for the safety of its employees, Shell shut down its operations in Ogoniland later that year.

Prompted by this loss of revenue, as well as a desire to reduce MOSOP's power, Nigeria's military government stepped up its campaign of terror against the protesters. A new dictator, General Sami Abacha, abolished all democratic institutions, closed down the newspapers, restricted the activities of foreign journalists, and threw many opposition leaders in jail. He also sent troops into Ogoniland to restore order. The troops consisted of members of rival ethnic groups, whom he felt would have little sympathy for the Ogoni cause. International human rights organizations reported hundreds of incidents of murder, torture, rape, imprisonment without trial, and destruction of property in Ogoni villages during this time. In fact, at least 27 Ogoni villages have been destroyed since 1993, leaving 2,000 people dead and another 80,000 homeless. The government claimed that it was forced to act in response to MOSOP's increasingly violent protests.

Meanwhile, Saro-Wiwa struggled to maintain control of his evolving organization. The radical youth wing, which tended to be poorer and less educated than MOSOP's founders, began to resent the educated elite. "MOSOP was changing the traditional structure," explained Saro-Wiwa's brother, Dr. David Owens Wiwa. "Those who benefitted from the old establishment, from government contracts, were seen as depriving the people of their due." The traditional chiefs of Ogoniland, in turn, wanted to distance themselves from the radicals, since they had more to lose in openly defying the military government with violent protests. Saro-Wiwa tried to mend the growing rift between the two sides, but some claimed that his passionate speeches only incited the youth wing of MOSOP toward more violence.

In May 1994, a secret government memo surfaced that increased the fear and tension among the members of MOSOP. "Shell operations still impossible unless ruthless military operations are undertaken for smooth economic activities to progress," Major Paul Okuntimo of the Nigerian security force wrote of the situation in Ogoniland. He went on to recommend "wasting targets cutting across communities and leadership cadres, especially vocal individuals of various groups." A rumor also circulated that the government was receiving money from the oil companies to finance additional military operations in the region. "This is it," Saro-Wiwa stated after reading the secret memo. "They are going to arrest us all and execute us. All for Shell."

SENTENCED TO DEATH

On May 21, 1994, a series of events was set into motion that ultimately fulfilled Saro-Wiwa's prediction. That day, the chief of the Ogoni village of Giokoo hosted a meeting of 100 traditional chiefs and other members of the educated elite. Members of the MOSOP radical youth movement viewed the gathering with suspicion, worrying that the chiefs might be planning to ally themselves with the government. In reaction to this perceived threat, 2,000 MOSOP radicals surrounded and attacked the Giokoo chief's palace while the meeting was in progress, killing four traditional chiefs who had broken their ties with the organization and wounding many other people. Despite the fact that Saro-Wiwa was not among the protesters and apparently did not find out about the murders until later, some people blamed him for the attack. "Rousing the Ogoni masses from passivity and despair, Saro-Wiwa had filled them with a sense of entitlement and rancor toward the old order," Joshua Hammer noted in *Harper's*. "He may have been miles from the scene of the killings in Giokoo, but he was, in some way, responsible."

The next day, government troops stormed into Ogoniland, arresting Saro-Wiwa and 14 other MOSOP activists. Then the forces reportedly went on a rampage, killing and raping hundreds of people. Saro-Wiwa and the others were held in custody for almost a year before they were formally charged with inciting the killings at Giokoo. During this time, they were periodically starved and tortured, and they were not allowed to see their families. Finally, in May 1995, the group was brought to trial before a military tribunal. Several former MOSOP officials testified against Saro-Wiwa, claiming that he had ordered his followers to murder the traditional chiefs, but journalists present noted that all the testimony sounded phony and rehearsed. Before long, two of the most important witnesses admitted that they had been bribed by the government to lie about Saro-Wiwa's role in the Giokoo tragedy.

In the middle of the proceedings, Saro-Wiwa's team of lawyers resigned from the case in anger, claiming that their client had no chance of receiving a fair trial. Saro-Wiwa sat calmly throughout the case and refused to look at the witnesses against him. "These people are criminals. They're going to find me guilty," he stated. "So I don't even bother to listen to the testimony. I'm not going to let these goons have any advantage over me." At the conclusion of the trial, Saro-Wiwa and eight of the other activists were found guilty and sentenced to death by hanging, without any opportunity to appeal the verdict.

After his conviction, Saro-Wiwa made the following statement: "My lord, we all stand before history. I am a man of peace, of ideas. Appalled by the denigrating poverty of my people who live on a richly endowed land, distressed by their political marginalization and economic strangulation, angered by the devastation of their land, their ultimate heritage, anxious to preserve their right to life and to a decent living, and determined to usher to this country as a whole a fair and just democratic system which protects everyone and every ethnic group and gives us all a valid claim to human civilization, I have devoted my intellectual and material resources, my very life, to a cause in which I have total belief and from which I cannot be blackmailed or intimidated. I have no doubt at all about the ultimate success of my cause, no matter the trials and tribulation which I and those who believe with me may encounter on our journey. No imprisonment nor death can stop our ultimate victory."

Saro-Wiwa's death sentence quickly drew worldwide attention. Environmental groups, human-rights advocates, and many national governments appealed to the Nigerian dictator to commute the sentence and release the "MOSOP nine." They also prevailed upon Shell to exert its considerable influence over the military government on behalf of Saro-Wiwa. After all, the oil company contributed about half of Nigeria's $10 billion in annual revenues. But Shell, for a variety of reasons, refused to get involved. "Businesses shouldn't be in the business of being political," one corporate spokesperson said. "We can't issue a bold statement because we have 4,500 employees there. It could be considered treasonous by the regime and the employees could come under attack. It would only inflame the issues." At the same time, however, Dr. Owens Wiwa claimed that the head of Shell's Nigerian operations had secretly approached him and offered to arrange for his brother's release under certain conditions. "He said he would be able to help us get Ken freed if we stopped the protest campaign abroad," Wiwa stated. "I was very shocked. Even if I had wanted to, I didn't have the power to control the international environmental protests."

Despite the worldwide outpouring of support, Ken Saro-Wiwa and the eight other activists were executed by Nigeria's military government in the early morning hours of November 10, 1995. According to reports, Saro-Wiwa remained calm and tried to comfort the other condemned men prior to his death. Sadly, it apparently took the executioners several attempts to hang him, since the pit beneath the gallows was not deep enough for the fall to break his neck. During this terrible ordeal, he managed to utter the last words: "Lord, take my soul, but the struggle continues."

AFTERMATH

As news of the executions spread through Ogoniland, thousands of people wandered out into the streets, many of them crying uncontrollably. Within a few hours, however, the government sent 4,000 troops into the region to forcibly prevent people from expressing their grief. "If the military sees two or three people gathering, they may imprison them. If you wear black, they may beat you," a teacher in an Ogoni village related. "If you carry newspapers, they will seize them. Our headmaster was arrested last week as a warning to us not to discuss Ken in the classroom. Pastors were arrested because they prayed for Ken Saro-Wiwa. They take people away every day." Despite the efforts of the government, though, many people privately noted that Saro-Wiwa had become a martyr in the eyes of his people.

"Ken's name is on the lips of every Ogoni child," one activist claimed. "The Ogonis will mourn him for generations."

The executions sparked an enormous reaction outside of Nigeria, as well. The United States, Canada, South Africa, and many European countries immediately recalled their ambassadors from Nigeria in protest. Some nations discussed imposing economic sanctions, such as an oil embargo, on Nigeria. International environmental and human rights groups launched a worldwide boycott of Shell—which was still going strong nearly a year later—and bombarded the company's headquarters with angry letters and faxes.

In an attempt to counteract the bad publicity Saro-Wiwa's death had generated, General Abacha hired several American public-relations firms. They placed advertisements in prominent newspapers around the world that blamed Saro-Wiwa and MOSOP for the violence in Ogoniland. Meanwhile, Shell tried to make amends by tripling the amount of money it had previously spent on building schools, hospitals, and other improvements for the people of the region. It also announced some new steps toward reducing the pollution created by its Nigerian operations, including plans to build a $3.8 billion natural gas processing plant in the Niger Delta. "Abacha had taken a calculated gamble" in proceeding with the executions, Hammer wrote. "The dictator surely knew the killings would disgust the world and possibly provoke sanctions. Yet, for Abacha, international [disgrace] was a fair exchange for internal stability."

Despite the steps taken by Shell and the Nigerian government, however, Saro-Wiwa's message did not seem likely to fade away. "When, after years of writing, I decided to take the Word to the streets to mobilize the Ogoni people and empower them to protest the devastation of their environment by Shell and their denigration and dehumanization by Nigeria's military dictators, I had no doubt where it could end," Saro-Wiwa wrote in a message smuggled out of his prison cell shortly before his death. "Whether I live or die is immaterial. It is enough to know that there are people who commit time, money and energy to fight this one evil among so many others predominating worldwide. If they do not succeed today, they will succeed tomorrow. We must keep on striving to make the world a better place for all mankind. Each one contributing his bit, in his or her own way. I salute you all." By mid-1996, MOSOP's example had encouraged the formation of at least 12 similar groups in other parts of Nigeria.

MARRIAGE AND FAMILY

Saro-Wiwa was married to a woman named Maria, and they had several children. One of Saro-Wiwa's sons, Ken Wiwa, has continued his work as an activist, traveling throughout Europe to raise awareness of the plight of the Ogoni. Saro-Wiwa's brother, Dr. David Owens Wiwa, also gives lectures around the world in support of the cause.

SELECTED WRITINGS

Songs in a Time of War, 1985
Sozaboy: A Novel in Rotten English, 1985
A Forest of Flowers, 1986
Basi and Company: A Modern African Folktale, 1987
Prisoners of Jebs, 1988
Adaku and Other Stories, 1989
Four Farcical Plays, 1989
On a Darkling Plain: An Account of the Nigerian Civil War, 1989
Nigeria: The Brink of Disaster, 1991
Similia: Essays on Anomic Nigeria, 1991
The Singing Anthill: Ogoni Folktales, 1991
Genocide in Nigeria: The Ogoni Tragedy, 1992

HONORS AND AWARDS

Goldman Environmental Prize: 1995

FURTHER READING

BOOKS

Contemporary Authors, Vol. 142
Saro-Wiwa, Ken. *Genocide in Nigeria: The Ogoni Tragedy,* 1992

PERIODICALS

Canadian Dimension, May-June 1996, p.45
Environmental Action, Winter 1996, p.6
Harper's, June 1996, p.58; Sep. 1996, p.20
Los Angeles Times, Apr. 17, 1995, p.E2
National Review, July 10, 1995, p.51
New Statesman and Society, Nov. 17, 1995, p.14
New York Times, Nov. 11, 1995, p.A1; Nov. 29, 1995, p.C18; Dec. 17, 1995, p.A11
New Yorker, Nov. 27, 1995, p.51
Newsweek, Nov. 20, 1995, p.64; Dec. 18, 1995, p.47
The Progressive, Jan. 1996, p.13
Sierra, Mar.-Apr. 1996, p.30
Wall Street Journal, Nov. 11, 1996, p.A9

Paul Watson   1950-
Canadian "Earth Warrior"
Founder of the Sea Shepherd Conservation Society

BIRTH

Paul Watson was born in Toronto, Ontario, Canada, on December 2, 1950. At the time of his birth, his father was stationed overseas as a soldier in the Korean War. When his father returned home in 1955, the family moved to a small fishing village in New Brunswick, on Canada's east coast. Watson was the oldest of six children.

YOUTH

Growing up near the Atlantic Ocean, Watson developed an early love for the outdoors and wildlife. As a boy, he enjoyed going on fishing trips and visiting a nearby marine biology station. One summer, he discovered a quiet pond where he would swim every day in the company of a beaver. "I think the fact that when I went back the next summer and couldn't find that beaver or any beavers and I found out that the trappers had taken them all was what radicalized me," he stated.

At his mother's suggestion, Watson joined an organization called the Kindness Club at the age of eight. The group's motto was "Be Kind," and its primary goal was "To foster the concept that animals, as well as people, have certain inalienable rights, including protection from cruelty." He took his responsibility as a member of the Kindness Club very seriously and made it his personal mission to prevent cruelty to animals. For example, he often roamed through the woods and released animals from hunters' traps. When he was 12, Watson convinced his father to buy him a BB gun, like most of the other kids in his neighborhood had, and then used it to enforce the rules of the Kindness Club. "That was the beginning of my career," he recalled. "I used to shoot kids. I'd shoot kids in the butt when they shot birds."

After Watson's mother died in 1963, the family moved to London, Ontario. Upset by his mother's death and unhappy about the move, Watson began having major conflicts with his father. He first attempted to run away from home at 14, but his father found him. The next year, however, he boarded a train heading west across Canada. He wound up in Vancouver, on the Pacific Ocean, where he soon joined the crew of a Norwegian merchant marine ship. Spending the next few years at sea gave Watson the opportunity to learn about running a ship and to visit exotic ports all over the world."Some of those clubs in South Africa!" he remembered. "I don't know how I got out alive." After returning to Vancouver, he served for a time in the Canadian Coast Guard. In between his adventures at sea, Watson spent one semester at Simon Fraser University in Canada studying communications.

CHOOSING A CAREER

In 1970, Watson joined a group of student-activists from Vancouver in protesting against the American testing of nuclear weapons on Amchitka Island, off the coast of Alaska. The protesters were angry about the environmental destruction that the testing would cause, as well as the possibility that developing such weapons might increase the likelihood of a nuclear war. The group took the radical step of hiring boats to take them to the island, placing themselves in the way of the explosion so that they would be killed if the tests proceeded as scheduled. The tests were delayed for several months due to technical problems, but they eventually did take place after the protesters had left.

Despite their lack of success on this first crusade, the group continued to exist and soon became known as Greenpeace. They also changed their focus from fighting the development of nuclear weapons to protecting the Earth's creatures and environment against humankind's harmful practices. It was clear from the beginning that Greenpeace activists were willing to use unconventional means to draw attention to their concerns. As a founding member of Greenpeace, Watson participated in many highly visible and controversial campaigns over the next few years—often risking his life for the cause. For example, he was on the crew of a Zodiac boat (a small, rubber pontoon boat with an outboard motor) that deliberately placed itself between a group of whales and a huge whaling ship that was trying to harpoon them. He also traveled to the Arctic Circle to help spray harp seal pups with an organic dye that would make their fur worthless to hunters.

Watson's own deep concern for animals and the environment gained focus in 1973. He obtained what he described as his "education as a warrior" that year when he joined a group of Native Americans engaged in a heated conflict with the U.S. government. Members of the American Indian Movement (AIM) occupied Wounded Knee, South Dakota—the site where 200 Sioux had been massacred by federal troops in 1890—to demand more land and rights for their people. The FBI and the National Guard soon surrounded the AIM activists. Watson crawled in the snow on his stomach to get through the blockade and served as a medic with AIM for the duration of the 71-day standoff. Afterward, the Oglala Sioux tribe recognized him as a warrior, giving him the Indian name Grey Wolf Clear Water. During the initiation ceremony in a sweat lodge, Watson had a vision that told him to dedicate his life to saving whales and other marine animals.

This experience confirmed Watson's decision to make his career as an "Earth warrior." "I intend to change the world. I believe . . . that any single person can make a difference if he allows his passion to be expressed through action. My passion is the living Earth, especially her oceans. I am a conservationist, a protector of species and ecological systems, and a defender of the rights of nature," he stated. "I am a warrior and it is the way of the warrior to fight against superior odds even when victory is no more than a dream. I have no illusions. I know that the rate of extinction on this Earth increases daily. This knowledge makes me angry. As a warrior, I cherish my anger, because it is anger that gives me courage and strengthens my resolve. The spectre of extinction, the prospect of diminishment, the certainty of a biological holocaust makes me strong."

CAREER HIGHLIGHTS

BREAKING WITH GREENPEACE

Encouraged by his vision, Watson became more active than ever in Greenpeace campaigns over the next few years. Gradually, however, some members of the organization began to feel that his views and actions were too radical. At the same time, Watson started to become frustrated with what he saw as the passive direction of the organization. The conflict came to a head in 1977, during an effort to disrupt the annual slaughter of baby harp seals in northern Canada. As one hunter prepared to club a baby seal on the head to take its valuable white pelt, Watson grabbed the club out of his hand and threw it into the freezing-cold ocean. This action violated a Canadian law against interfering with the seal hunt, and Greenpeace officials also claimed that it broke the group's rule against using violence. Watson ended up being thrown out of Greenpeace. He soon decided that the parting of ways was for the best, however, given his growing philosophical differences with the organization.

"When we set up Greenpeace it was because we wanted a small group of action-oriented people who could get into the field and . . . make an issue controversial and publicize it and get to the root of the problem," Watson noted. "That was fine for the first seven years or so. We were successful at doing that. And then we woke up." He felt that as Greenpeace grew, its leaders became too concerned about raising money and gaining respectability to continue with the organization's original mission. By the mid-1990s, Greenpeace was the largest environmental group in the world, with 5 million members. It also had 1,000 paid employees, two-thirds of whom worked primarily on fund-raising activities. Still hoping to make a difference through direct confrontation, Watson decided it was time to form his own group.

SEA SHEPHERD CONSERVATION SOCIETY

Watson called his new organization the Sea Shepherd Conservation Society. Its purpose was to use whatever means necessary to stop the destruction of marine wildlife and ocean habitat due to the illegal or unethical practices of humans. In the process, the Sea Shepherds hoped to raise public awareness of the situation on the high seas. "One of the things we do is dramatic confrontation. The more dramatic you can make it, the more controversial it is, the more exposure you will get," Watson explained. "If you've got film of it, all the better. The drama translates into exposure. Then you tie the message into that exposure and fire it into the brains of millions of people."

Despite his willingness to use controversial tactics to get the point across, Watson claimed that Sea Shepherd activities were based on the teachings of Hindu spiritual leader Mahatma Gandhi, who advocated nonviolent protest. Though the Sea Shepherds frequently destroy property that is used to harm marine life, they go to great lengths to avoid injuring humans in the process. Watson described the guiding principles of his organization: "One is that we don't use firearms. Two, we don't utilize explosives. Three, we don't take any action where there is the possibility of injury to somebody. Four, we accept responsibility for what we do. And, five, we accept whatever moral or legal consequences will befall."

With the help of some friends in the anti-hunting group Fund for Animals, Watson was able to buy his first boat—an old North Atlantic trawler that he re-outfitted and named the *Sea Shepherd*—in 1979. That spring, he took the ship on its first mission: to the North Atlantic, off Labrador, to disrupt the annual seal hunt in a highly confrontational way. Worried about what form the protests might take, Canadian authorities sent the Royal Mounted Police to keep the situation under control.

After crossing miles of ice to reach the scene of the hunt, Watson was ready to place himself in danger for the cause. "I handcuffed myself to the winchline that hauls pelts across the ice," he recalled. "I thought it was a good idea, with all those police around. That would protect me. The trouble was, they just winched me across the ice, through the water, and up the side of the ship. They dragged me through this gauntlet of sealers, who were kicking and spitting on me." The police did nothing to stop the assault, and instead placed Watson—by that time semi-conscious from repeated dunkings in the frigid ocean—under arrest. His case eventually went all the way to the Canadian Supreme Court, where the law forbidding citizens from protesting against the seal hunt was found to be an unconstitutional restriction on civil liberties in 1983.

THE SINKING OF THE *SIERRA*

Free pending his hearing, Watson took his ship on another dangerous crusade later that year, when the Sea Shepherds went in search of the notorious pirate whaling ship *Sierra*. "Pirate whalers" are boats that roam the oceans of the world killing every whale they can find—regardless of their size or species, and in flagrant violation of international law. They often fly the flag of a country that does not participate in the International Whaling Commission (IWC), which regulates the number and type of whales that can be harvested each year by its members. The whale meat, oil, and bones from illegal whaling activities are most frequently sold in Japan, where they are used to make exotic foods and traditional medicines.

Watson and his crew found the *Sierra* anchored off the coast of Portugal, where it was waiting for a Japanese freighter to arrive so that it could unload its illegal cargo. They decided to use the *Sea Shepherd* to ram the pirate

whaler, hoping to sink it and put the whaling operation out of business. After contacting the *Sierra*'s captain by radio to identify himself and warn of his intentions, Watson cranked the *Sea Shepherd* up to top speed and smashed into the middle of the rival ship, ripping a 10-foot hole in its side. Then he turned around and rammed the pirate whaler again, creating a 40-foot hole that exposed the whale meat inside. As the *Sierra* managed to start its engines and limp toward the nearby port of Leixoes, Watson turned the *Sea Shepherd* around and fled up the coast. A few hours later, just eight miles before he would have reached the safety of Spanish territorial waters, his ship was caught by a destroyer from the Portuguese Navy and forced to return to Leixoes.

The Portuguese authorities seemed confused about what to do with Watson once he got there. They threatened to charge him with operating his vessel in a reckless manner, but he insisted that his actions could not be considered reckless since he had fully intended to ram the *Sierra*. Hoping to draw international attention to Portugal's role in supporting illegal whaling activities, Watson demanded to be arrested. In the end, however, the Portuguese authorities deported him from the country and impounded the *Sea Shepherd*. They later informed Watson that he would have to pay a fine of $750,000 to get his boat back; otherwise, it would be given to the owners of the *Sierra* as compensation for the damage he had inflicted on their ship.

Watson refused to pay the fine, which was several times more than the boat was worth. Instead of allowing the *Sea Shepherd* to fall into the hands of the pirates, he decided to return to Portugal secretly and sink it. "We decided that New Year's Eve was the best time," he noted. "We thought we'd never get another chance. Everyone was partying. Everything was slack. At ten that night, [fellow Sea Shepherd] Peter Woof and I opened the sea cocks [giant valves that let in seawater to cool the engines]. It was like turning on six high-powered fire hydrants." The boat filled with water and sank to the bottom of the Leixoes harbor within about three hours. Later that night, as Watson tried to make his escape, he nearly got caught. Jumping into a taxi, he told the Portuguese-speaking driver to take him to the airport. The driver misunderstood and took him back to the port. "I saw the bow of the *Sea Shepherd* sticking out of the water, and the place was full of armed guards with machine guns," Watson recalled. "When we finally got to the plane, I just walked on. The guard at the checkpoint didn't even look at my name."

PROTECTING WHALES

Watson continued his efforts to protect whales from illegal slaughter through the next decade. Though increasingly strict limits were placed on whaling by the IWC over these years, the Sea Shepherds found and exposed many violations of the law. In 1981, Watson took his new boat, *Sea Shepherd II*, to Siberia, where he filmed citizens of the Soviet Union illegally killing whales and using the meat as feed on mink farms. A Soviet destroyer and two helicopter gunships chased the *Sea Shepherd II* out to sea, but Watson refused their orders to halt, escaped to international waters, and turned the incriminating film over to the IWC.

In 1985, the Sea Shepherds took their whale-saving campaign to the Faeroe Islands, a Danish-held territory near the Arctic Circle between Scotland and Iceland. Endangered pilot whales passed close by the islands at the same time every year on their migration route, and island residents turned the event into an annual slaughter. They herded the whales into shallow water, where they became stuck. Then groups of people, including children, circled around the whales and hacked them to death with machetes. The Faeroese government claimed that the *Grind*, as the event was known, did not violate international whaling laws because it was a traditional hunt undertaken by indigenous people.

But Watson noted that the hunt was not really necessary to feed the Faeroese people: the country enjoyed one of the highest standards of living in the world, and every year more than twice as many whales were killed than were eaten. "The whales are killed for sport and because it is a tradition," he stated. "The *Grind* is a primitive orgy of blood and violence, the ultimate expression of human contempt for nature." On their first trip to the Faeroes, the Sea Shepherds saved many whales by using their boat to turn the migration route farther from the islands. When they returned to port, the crew was pelted with rotten eggs by angry Faeroese people. The next year, Watson returned to the islands with a film crew from the British Broadcasting Corporation (BBC) and recorded part of the annual slaughter. As they tried to leave, however, the *Sea Shepherd II* was intercepted by a Faeroese patrol boat, which fired shotguns and tear gas at Watson and his crew while the BBC filmed the whole thing. The story became a dramatic BBC television movie, *Black Harvest*, that provoked public outrage around the world.

TARGETING DRIFT-NET FISHERMEN

In the late 1980s, after the IWC enacted a worldwide ban on whaling, Watson turned his attention to the growing problem of drift-net fishing in the world's oceans. Drift nets are enormous nets — up to 35 miles long — with floats at the top and weights at the bottom. Commercial fishing boats drag such nets through the ocean in a giant circle to trap valuable food species like tuna and squid. According to Watson, however, this type of fishing not only dangerously depletes the numbers of the target species, but also kills a lot of other marine life that happens to become entangled in the nets. In fact, billions of fish are caught this way each year, along with 250,000 marine mammals (like seals and dolphins) and more than a million seabirds. "The more fish they get, the fewer fish there are. The fewer fish there are, the more elaborate the technology. They're not concerned about the future. They're only concerned about getting the maximum profit in the shortest period of time," he stated. "It's a global systematic assault on the biology of the oceans."

In 1988, the Sea Shepherds took gruesome photographs to document the large number of dolphins that were killed during the daily operations of an American ship that used seine nets to catch tuna. This footage helped raise public awareness of the problem and contributed to a regulation mandating that only tuna caught using dolphin-safe methods could be sold in U.S. markets. In 1992, Watson took two boats into the Pacific to disrupt illegal drift-net fishing activities. They collected miles worth of drift net and halted the operations of a Japanese ship by throwing capsules containing smelly butyric acid onto its decks.

CONFLICT WITH OTHER ENVIRONMENTALISTS

Because of his confrontational tactics, Watson has been called a "terrorist" by his enemies, and even by a few of his allies. Some environmental activists feel that Watson's approach often backfires, giving environmentalists a bad name and making negotiation more difficult. "You can't be too concerned with what people call you and you can't be too concerned about people's attitudes," he responded. "All you can do is be true to yourself: you don't kill anybody, you don't injure anybody, you do everything you can to save as many lives and as much habitat as you possibly can. If you do that, then you're doing the right thing."

Others admire Watson for repeatedly putting his life on the line to protect the creatures of the sea. "I don't want to be alive in a world that has destroyed itself. I couldn't live in a world without whales and seals. So I'm doing this for myself, for my own survival," he stated. "I fully expect to be killed one day by one of my own species. A whaler, sealer, shark poacher or member of the crew on a drift-netter or drag trawler will kill me. Or it may be a government agent acting as the hired thug of a corporation. But the only thing that matters to me is that I use my life to save lives, protect species and conserve habitat. By doing so, I know that I can make a difference, and perhaps inspire others who will also make a difference. . . . My work may amount to no more than a ripple on the ocean's surface. But there have been others who have made ripples before me. . . . My own ripple will join theirs, and together they will become wavelets and waves, and eventually, perhaps, thundering surf crashing upon the rocks of human ignorance and selfishness."

"For more than 20 years I have tried to make the world a little better for those who will inherit it," he continued. "I have been both a strategist and a tactician for the environmental movement. I have made friends and enemies. I cherish both. My enemies are a challenge, my friends a source of strength. To some I am a hero. To others I am a pirate, a villain, even a terrorist. The qualities that make me appear heroic to some also make me appear piratical to others. All heroes have enemies; the greater the hero, the greater, stronger and more numerous the enemies. I look forward to cultivating many more enemies in my career on behalf of the Earth."

MARRIAGE AND FAMILY

Watson's first marriage, to a Chinese-Canadian woman named Starlet, ended in divorce. In 1992, he married Lisa Distefano, who shares his concerns about marine life and is very active in Sea Shepherd campaigns. When he is not at sea on an environmental mission, Watson lives in Vancouver, Canada.

WRITINGS

Ocean Warrior: My Battle to End the Illegal Slaughter on the High Seas, 1994
Earthforce! An Earth Warrior's Guide to Strategy, 1994

FURTHER READING

BOOKS

Morris, David B. *Earth Warrior: Overboard with Paul Watson and the Sea Shepherd Conservation Society,* 1995
Scarce, Rik. *Eco-Warriors: Understanding the Radical Environmental Movement,* 1990
Watson, Paul. *Ocean Warrior: My Battle to End the Illegal Slaughter on the High Seas,* 1994

PERIODICALS

The Animals' Agenda, May-June 1994, p.14
Atlantic, Nov. 1980, p.65
Audubon, May 1982, p.32
E, Nov.-Dec. 1995, p.36
Interview, Aug. 1992, p.94
Maclean's, June 16, 1980, p.13
Omni, Feb. 1981, p.16
U.S. News and World Report, Nov. 24, 1986, p.72
Whole Life Times, Apr. 1996, p.20

ADDRESS

Sea Shepherd Conservation Society
3107A Washington Blvd.
Marina del Ray, CA 90292

WORLD WIDE WEB SITE

http://www.seashepherd.org
http://www2.seashepherd.org/orgs/sscs

Adam Werbach   1973-
American Environmental Activist
Founder of Sierra Student Coalition
Youngest President of Sierra Club

BIRTH

Adam Werbach was born on January 15, 1973, in Tarzana, California. His father, Mel Werbach, is a psychiatrist, while his mother, Gayle Werbach, is an educational therapist. He also has an older brother, Kevin.

YOUTH

Werbach involved himself in environmental activism at a very young age. In 1981, when he was eight years old, he saw a letter addressed to his parents from the Sierra Club, America's oldest and best-known environmental organization. The letter urged his parents to join the group in calling for the resignation of James Watt, who was the Secretary of the Interior at that time. As head of the Department of Interior, Watt was responsible for protecting America's wilderness, but environmentalists felt that many of his proposals actually posed a great threat to the country's forests, rivers, lakes, and wildlife.

After looking over the letter, young Werbach was still a little unsure about why everyone was so unhappy with Watt, but he took the recall petition that was included in the letter to his second grade class the next day. After getting permission from his teacher, he went from class to class, asking his fellow students to sign the recall petition. By the end of the day, Werbach's petition had nearly 200 signatures on it. His little one-boy petition drive planted the seeds of his enduring interest in environmental activism and the conservation efforts of the Sierra Club.

As he grew older, Werbach's love for the wilderness blossomed. The area in which his family lived during his childhood was "mostly orange orchards and horse farms," he recalled, so there were still a lot of fields and woods for him to play in. Family hiking trips to national parks around the West also contributed to his appreciation for wilderness. But it was not until he was a teenager, when he read a book about legendary environmentalist David Brower (see entry in this volume of *Biography Today*), that Werbach felt the pull of conservation activism. Brower's life and achievements inspired him, and Werbach subsequently began to voice his feelings about environmental issues with increased passion and conviction. "He's my hero," Werbach said about Brower. "He's the reason I made the choice to be in the Sierra Club."

EDUCATION

Werbach attended high school at Harvard-Westlake School, a private institution in North Hollywood. In his junior year, though, he attended the Mountain School of Milton Academy in Vermont. The Mountain School ran a program that taught students about environmental issues, in addition to the usual school subjects.

During his high school days, Werbach was known among his fellow students at Harvard-Westlake for his interest in conservation. A dedicated vegetarian who started an animal rights study group at the school, he spent much of his free time in 1990 organizing students on behalf of "Big Green." Big Green was a comprehensive set of proposed changes designed to strengthen state environmental laws and measures. Big Green was eventually defeated by California voters, but Werbach's small organization of ecology-minded students stayed alive. The group was transformed into an early chapter of the Sierra Student Coalition (SSC), a student environmental organization.

After graduating from high school in 1990, Werbach attended Brown University, where he continued his conservation work. He also pursued an ambitious schedule of classwork and other extracurricular activities. He was the lead baritone for the school's Brown Derbies, an *a cappela* (without instrumental support) singing group that toured the world and released two CDS. Werbach also produced and directed several films and videos during his time at Brown. During the early 1990s, he even managed to secure an advanced degree in Spanish from the Instituto Central America of Guatemala. In December 1995 Werbach graduated with bachelor's degrees in political science and modern culture and media.

After graduating from Brown, Werbach was accepted to Columbia University's graduate program for film studies. He delayed his entrance into the school, though, for by this time his enthusiastic activism on behalf of the environment had gained the attention of some of the most important people in the U.S. conservationist community. When he realized that he had an opportunity to become a leading voice in the Sierra Club, Werbach decided that Columbia could wait.

CAREER HIGHLIGHTS

SIERRA STUDENT COALITION

Back in 1990, Werbach had emerged as a leader of the Sierra Student Coalition, an organization of environmentally concerned students such as the ones who had worked on behalf of Big Green in California. Sponsored by the Sierra Club, which had long wanted to establish a national student program as part of its activist network, the SSC grew rapidly. It registered thousands of student voters, trained hundreds of student activists, and encouraged students all over the country to pay attention to environmental issues.

The leadership of the Sierra Club was very impressed with Werbach's leadership of the SSC. The group — which grew to 30,000 members during Werbach's tenure as director — showed great energy and grit in its activities. In 1994, in fact, the efforts of one SSC chapter helped secure passage of the California Desert Protection Act.

The California Desert Protection Act was intended to protect millions of acres of wilderness in the California desert. Some legislators in the U.S. Congress wanted to keep the area open for mining and development, though, so they tried to block it. The Massachusetts chapter of the SSC was determined to see that the bill passed, but they knew that the Senate vote on the act was going to be close. The students quickly organized a campaign in which a barrage of telephone calls were directed at Senator John

Kerry of Massachusetts. Kerry favored the legislation, but he was going to miss the vote on the bill because of a holiday vacation that he had planned. As the phone calls poured into his office, though, Kerry changed his mind and stayed in Washington, D.C., to cast his vote on the bill. His vote proved to be the difference between victory and defeat. The California Desert Protection Act passed by one vote, thus ensuring the protection of millions of acres of California wilderness. That vote would not have been cast if the high school and college students of the Sierra Student Coalition had not sprung into action.

PRESIDENT OF THE SIERRA CLUB

In 1994, while still a 21-year-old college student, Werbach became the youngest person ever elected to the Sierra Club's Board of Directors. As a member of the club's governing body, he continued to impress older members of the organization such as his idol, David Brower. As 1996 elections for some of the organization's leadership positions drew near, Brower and others encouraged Werbach to run for the presidency of the club. "What we should be doing now is thinking about what we want the club and the country to look like 50 years from now," said Brower, who first became associated with the Sierra Club in the 1930s. "We need a new generation of leaders."

Supporters of Werbach's candidacy pointed out that the average age of a Sierra Club member was 47. Even though many young people are concerned about environmental issues, they often do not get involved with organized efforts to protect wilderness or stop polluters. These supporters argued that young leaders like Werbach could help the Sierra Club to gather new allies among the under-30 crowd in America. "Young people are the most supportive [of environmentalism] and the least engaged," remarked Carl Pope, the club's executive director. "Adam's campaign platform was that he was really going to reach out to his generation and mobilize them for the '96 elections."

In May 1996 Werbach was elected president of the Sierra Club at the age of 23. His election surprised some people, but supporters pointed out that he had more than just youth going for him. "If [Werbach's election] were only symbolic, it wouldn't be enough," said a member of the Natural Resources Defense Council. "Adam has not only youth and energy but commitment and passion and experience." Brower agreed, saying "it's amazing to me to find someone with the environmental sense he's got and the social grace as well."

For his part, Werbach made it clear that he was excited about the upcoming challenges he would face. "The Sierra Club is now in its second century of protecting America's environment, for our families and for our future," he said when his election was announced. "It's time my generation

Adam Werbach with his idol David Brower

stepped up, acted on our environmental values, and joined forces with the Sierra Club to protect our air, water, and wild places."

Werbach's election triggered a wave of media attention for himself and the Sierra Club. National magazines and large newspapers did feature stories on him, and even David Letterman expressed interest in having him appear on his show. But Werbach remained unfazed by all the publicity about the "boy wonder" who had assumed leadership of the Sierra Club. "If the primary purpose of the Sierra Club is to be concerned about the future, it seems natural that young people take responsibility for it," he said.

As president of the Sierra Club, Werbach is responsible for supervising the organization's paid staff and volunteer leaders, and helping coordinate the activities of the club's nearly 600,000 members. The length of Werbach's term is only one year, though he is eligible for re-election in 1997 if he decides to run. In addition, the presidency of the Sierra Club is an unpaid position; the only compensation he receives from the organization is a small amount of money for living expenses. But it was clear that the opportunity to make a difference was much more important to Werbach than pocketing a fat paycheck.

As Werbach settled into his new job, he made it clear that, in addition to taking care of his supervisory responsibilities, he planned to spend a lot of time encouraging young people to join the Sierra Club and to get involved in conservation efforts. "The environment is the primary issue that prompts this generation, my generation, to take social and political action," he noted. "Our job is to get the word out to them and to give them a place to act on their anxieties and convictions. My goal is to make that place the Sierra Club."

Werbach is convinced that he can reach young people by taking approaches that the Sierra Club has not previously explored. He contends that a huge audience friendly to the club's message is out there, and that the club can reach them through music, film, television, fashion, the Internet, and other aspects of popular culture. "It's not their job to come to us, it's our job to go to them. If they don't read our books then we need to go to MTV," he explained. "We have to show them politics is something positive, *exciting,* something they'll want to be *involved* in."

Werbach has wasted little time in pursuing his ideas for reaching young people. Even before becoming president, Werbach had helped the Sierra Club familiarize itself with the Internet and other new electronic media that are popular with teenagers and people in their 20s. In the weeks following his election, he began talking with executives at MTV about adding environmental reports to the channel's programming. He also wants the Sierra Club and MTV to collaborate on an environmental awareness campaign. "Expect concerts, expect albums, expect joint media events," Werbach said confidently.

ENVIRONMENTAL VIEWS

"The greatest environmental threat we face is political apathy," Werbach remarked in August 1996. He worries that Americans have become cynical and depressed about what the future holds for them and their families. But Werbach also believes that a renewed devotion to environmental protection can "reinvigorate our faith in the future, . . . reinvigorate the belief that, when I have kids, they'll inherit a world that is better than the one that I received. I never lost my faith in the future."

Werbach also believes that people will recognize the importance of protecting the environment and America's wilderness regions if they are educated about the forces that threaten them. "There are places that we need to protect because they're like museums," he said. "These are the last vestiges of our wild planet."

HOBBIES AND OTHER INTERESTS

Werbach has a wide range of interests that keep him very busy. He enjoys working on the computer, and he is a big fan of the Internet. A fine singer during his days at Brown, he plays occasional gigs as a member of a folk-funk band, Air. Werbach also likes to write; he has begun work on a novel called *Whirrled* with his brother, Kevin. In addition, Werbach plans to resume his study of filmmaking at Columbia sometime in the future.

HOME AND FAMILY

Werbach, who is not married, lives in San Francisco when he is not traveling on Sierra Club business.

HONORS AND AWARDS

"Environmental Hero" (Sierra Club): 1991

FURTHER READING

BOOKS

Brinkley, Douglas. *The Magic Bus*, 1993
Turner, Tom. *Sierra Club: 100 Years of Protecting Nature*, 1991

PERIODICALS

Interview, Sep. 1996, p.40
Los Angeles Times, May 27, 1996, p.E1
New York Times, June 2, 1996, p.N9
Newsweek, June 17, 1996, p.71
Outside, Sep. 1996, p.68
People, Sep. 16, 1996, p.65
The Planet, July/Aug. 1996, p.8
San Francisco Chronicle, May 25, 1996, p.A1
Sierra, Sep./Oct. 1996, p.54
Swing, Sep. 1996, p.82

Additional information was taken from Sierra Club publicity materials, and from a National Public Radio broadcast of a speech Werbach delivered in San Francisco on August 20, 1996.

ADDRESS

Sierra Club
85 Second Street, Second Floor
San Francisco, CA 94105-3441

WORLD WIDE WEB SITE

http://www.sierraclub.org

Photo and Illustration Credits

Appendix to Web Sites
for Environmental Groups

African Wildlife Foundation
http://www.awf.org/

Alaska Rainforest Campaign, The
http://www.akrain.org/

American Society of Primatologists
http://www.asp.org/

Americans for the Environment
http://www.ewg.org/pub/home/afe/
homepage.htm

Animals' Agenda, The
http://www.envirolink.org/arrs/aa/
index.html

Arctic National Wildlife Refuge
http://www.alaskan.com/anwr/

Bat Conservation International
http://www.batcon.org/

Bird Life International
http://www.surfnet.fi/birdlife/int/
bleng001.html

Brower, David
http://www.earthisland.org/ei/
brower/browerbr.html

Carson, Rachel
http://www.sirius.com/~fitch/wells/
carson/carson/.html
http://www.lm.com/~markt/rachel/
carson.html

**Committee for the National Institute for
the Environment, The**
http://www.cnie.org/

Conservation International
http://www.conservation.org/

Curriculum Safari Earth
http://cse2000.org/

Desert USA
http://www.desertusa.com/index.html

E TheEnvironment Magazine
http://www.emagazine.com/

EE Link — Endangered Species
http://www.nceet.snre.umich.edu/
EndSpp/Endangered.html

Earth First
http://www.imaja.com/imaja/change/
environment/ef/earthfirst.html

Earth Island Institute
http://www.earthisland.org/

Earth Share
http://www.earthshare.org/

Earth Watch International
http://www.earthwatch.org/

Ecology Action Center
http://www.cfn.cs.dal.ca/Environment/
EAC/EAC-Home.html

Ecotrust
http://www.ecotrust.org/

Endangered Species Recovery Program
http://arnica.csustan.edu/esrpp/
esrpp.htm

EnviroLink
http://www.envirolink.org/aboutel/

Environmental Defense Fund
http://www.edf.org/

Environmental Journals and Newsletters
http://www.lib.kth.se/~lg/ejourn.htm

Everglades Home Page, The
http://everglades.ycg.org/

Everglades National Park
http://taz.interpoint.net/~ahs/
Cyberfair96/GLADES.HTM

First Nation's Global Aboriginal Links
http://www.first-nations.com/
links01.html

Friends of the Earth
http://www.essential.org/orgs/FOE/
FOE.html

Gibbs, Lois
http://www.cais.net/wolf/cchw/
cchw.html

**Global Network of Environment and
Technology, The**
http://www.gnet.org/

Greenpeace
http://www.greenpeace.org/

Green Belt Movement
http://www.cous.uvic.ca/sscf/econ/
walter/DEVC002A.HTM

Internet Resources for Aboriginal, Torres Strait Islander and Indigenous Studies
http://www.unisa.edu.au/library/
internet/pathfind/abstu.htm

Jane Goodall Institute, The
http://www.gsn.org/gsn/proj/jgi/
index.html

League of Conservation Voters
http://www.lcv.org/

Links to Aboriginal Resources
http://www.bloorstreet.com/300block/
aborl.htm

Malibu Dolphin Recovery Center
http://elfi.com/mdrc.html

Mittermeier, Russell
http://www.conservation.org

National Audubon Society
http://www.audubon.org/audubon/

National Geographic Society
http://www.nationalgeographic.com/

National Geographic Magazine
http://www.nationalgeographic.com/
ngs/mags/ng_online/ngm_splash
001.html

National Park Service, The
http://www.nps.gov/

National Resources Defense Council
http://www.nrdc.org/nrdc/

National Wildlife Federation
http://www.nwf.org/international/

Nationwide Green Organizations in the USA (Green Party)
http://www.greens.org/usa/

Oregon National Desert Association
http://www.teleport.com/~onda/

Outdoor Life Magazine
http://www.outdoorlife.com/

Outside Magazine
http://outside.starwave.com/
magazine/omindex.html

Parrot Preservation Society
http://www.primenet.com/~macaws/

People for the Ethical Treatment of Animals
http://www.envirolink.org/arrs/peta/

Pesticide Action Network North America
http://www.panna.org/panna/

Peterson, Roger Tory
http://www.rtpt.org
http://www.petersononline.com

Quail Unlimited Home Page
http://www.outdoorsource.com/quail/

Rainforest Action Network
http://www.ran.org/ran/

Rainforest Alliance
http://www.rainforest-alliance.org/

Rainforest Relief
http://www.redbank.com/rrelief/

Save the Whales
http://www.tmarts.com/savethewhales/

Sea Shepherd Conservation Society
http://www2.seashepherd.org/

Sierra Club, The
http://www.sierraclub.org/

Species Survival Commission
http://w3.iprolink.ch/iucnlib/themes/
ssc/

Smithsonian Institution's Conservation and Research Center, The
http://www.si.edu/crc/

Southeast Alaska Conservation Council
http://www.juneau.com/seacc/
seacc.html

Southern Utah Wilderness Alliance
http://www.xmission.com/~suwa/
suwa.html

Tropical Rainforest Coalition
http://www.rainforest.org/

Tusk Trust, The
http://www.tusk.org/

U.S. Environmental Protection Agency
http://www.epa.gov/

U.S. Fish and Wildlife Service
http://www.fws.gov/

Watson, Paul
http://www2.seashepherd.org

Werbach, Adam, *see*
Adam Werbach Page, The
http://www.werbach.com/adam/
adam.html

WhaleNet
http://whale.wheelock.edu/

Whale Adoption Project
http://www.webcom.com/~iwcwww/
whale_adoption/waphome.html

Whole Earth Review
http://www.well.net/mwec/wer.html

Wild Dolphin Project, The
http://wwwa.com/dolphin/

Wilderness Society, The
http://www.wilderness.org/

WOLFSITE, The World of Wolves
http://www.wolfsite.com/

World Wide Fund for Nature
http://www.panda.org/

World-Wide-Web Virtual Library—
Herpetology
http://xtal200.harvard.edu:8000/herp/

World Wildlife Fund
http://www.wwf.org/

Yellowstone Journal
http://www.wyoming.com/
~yellowstonejournal/

Yellowstone National Park
http://www.nps.gov/yell/

Name Index

Listed below are the names of all individuals profiled in *Biography Today*, followed by the date of the issue in which they appear.

General Index

This index includes subjects, occupations, organizations, and ethnic and minority origins that pertain to individuals profiled in *Biography Today*.

Places of Birth Index

The following index lists the places of birth for the individuals profiled in *Biography Today*. Places of birth are entered under state, province, and/or country.

Kansas
Alley, Kirstie (Wichita). . . . . Jul 92
Dole, Bob (Russell). . . . . Jan 96
Parks, Gordon (Fort Scott) . . . . Artist 96
Sanders, Barry (Wichita). . . . . . . Sep 95
Kenya
Leakey, Louis (Nairobi) . . . . . Science 96
Maathai, Wangari (Nyeri) . . . . . . Env 97
Ndeti, Cosmas (Machakos) . . . . . Sep 95
Louisiana
Marsalis, Wynton
  (New Orleans) . . . . Apr 92
Roberts, Cokie (New Orleans) . . Apr 95
Maine
King, Stephen (Portland) . . . . Author 95
Maryland
Marshall, Thurgood (Baltimore) . . Jan 92
Ripken, Cal, Jr.
  (Havre de Grace). . . . . Sport 96
Massachusetts
Bush, George (Milton) . . . . Jan 92
Butcher, Susan (Cambridge). . . Sport 96
Cormier, Robert
  (Leominister) . . . . Author 95
Guey, Wendy (Boston) . . . . Sep 96
Guy, Jasmine (Boston) . . . . Sep 93
Kerrigan, Nancy (Woburn) . . . . . Apr 94
Pine, Elizabeth Michele (Boston) . . Jan 94
Scarry, Richard (Boston). . . . . . . Sep 94
Seuss, Dr. (Springfield) . . . . Jan 92
Speare, Elizabeth George
  (Melrose) . . . . Sep 95
Voigt, Cynthia (Boston) . . . . Oct 92
Walters, Barbara (Boston). . . . . . Sep 94
Mexico
Rivera, Diego (Guanajuato) . . . Artist 96
Michigan
Askins, Renee . . . . Env 97
Galeczka, Chris (Sterling
  Heights). . . . . Apr 96
Johnson, Magic (Lansing) . . . . . . Apr 92
Krone, Julie (Benton Harbor) . . . . Jan 95
Lalas, Alexi (Royal Oak). . . . . . . Sep 94
Van Allsburg, Chris . . . . Apr 92
Minas Gerais, Brazil
Pelé (Tres Coracoes). . . . . Sport 96
Minnesota
Burger, Warren (St. Paul) . . . . . . Sep 95
Douglas, Marjory Stoneman
  (Minneapolis) . . . . Env 97

Murie, Olaus J. . . . . Env 97
Paulsen, Gary (Minneapolis). . Author 95
Ryder, Winona (Winona) . . . . Jan 93
Schulz, Charles
  (Minneapolis) . . . . Author 96
Winfield, Dave (St. Paul). . . . . . . Jan 93
Mississippi
Brandy (McComb) . . . . Apr 96
Jones, James Earl (Arkabutla
  Township) . . . . Jan 95
Rice, Jerry (Crawford) . . . . Apr 93
Taylor, Mildred D. (Jackson). . Author 95
Winfrey, Oprah (Kosciusko) . . . . Apr 92
Missouri
Angelou, Maya (St. Louis). . . . . . Apr 93
Champagne, Larry III (St, Louis). . Apr 96
Goodman, John (Affton). . . . . Sep 95
Limbaugh, Rush (Cape
  Girardeau). . . . . Sep 95
Miller, Shannon (Rolla). . . . . Sep 94
Montana
Carvey, Dana (Missoula). . . . . . . Jan 93
Horner, Jack (Shelby) . . . . Science 96
Nevada
Agassi, Andre (Las Vegas). . . . . . Jul 92
New Jersey
Blume, Judy. . . . . Jan 92
Carpenter, Mary Chapin
  (Princeton). . . . . Sep 94
Earle, Sylvia (Gibbstown) . . . Science 96
Houston, Whitney (Newark). . . . Sep 94
Ice-T (Newark) . . . . Apr 93
Lawrence, Jacob
  (Atlantic City) . . . . Artist 96
Martin, Ann M. (Princeton) . . . . . Jan 92
O'Neal, Shaquille (Newark). . . . . Sep 93
Queen Latifah (Newark) . . . . Apr 92
Rodman, Dennis (Trenton) . . . . . Apr 96
Schwarzkopf, H. Norman
  (Trenton). . . . . Jan 92
Thomas, Dave (Atlantic City) . . . Apr 96
New Mexico
Foreman, Dave (Albuquerque). . . Env 97
New York State
Abdul-Jabbar, Kareem
  (New York City) . . . . Sport 96
Avi (New York City) . . . . Jan 93
Baldwin, James
  (New York City). . . . . Author 96
Blair, Bonnie (Cornwall) . . . . Apr 94

Birthday Index

January

1 Salinger, J.D. (1919)
2 Asimov, Isaac (1920)
4 Naylor, Phyllis Reynolds (1933)
Shula, Don (1930)
8 Hawking, Stephen W. (1942)
9 Menchu, Rigoberta (1959)
Nixon, Richard (1913)
12 Limbaugh, Rush (1951)
15 Werbach, Adam (1973)
16 Fossey, Dian (1932)
17 Carrey, Jim (1962)
Cormier, Robert (1925)
Jones, James Earl (1931)
18 Messier, Mark (1961)
19 Askins, Renee (1959)
Johnson, John (1918)
21 Domingo, Placido (1941)
Olajuwon, Hakeem (1963)
22 Chavis, Benjamin (1948)
23 Thiessen, Tiffani-Amber (1974)
25 Alley, Kirstie (1955)
28 Gretzky, Wayne (1961)
29 Abbey, Edward (1927)
Gilbert, Sara (1975)
Winfrey, Oprah (1954)
31 Ryan, Nolan (1947)

February

1 Spinelli, Jerry (1941)
Yeltsin, Boris (1931)
3 Nixon, Joan Lowery (1927)
Rockwell, Norman (1894)
4 Parks, Rosa (1913)
5 Aaron, Hank (1934)
6 Leakey, Mary (1913)
Zmeskal, Kim (1976)
7 Brooks, Garth (1962)
8 Grisham, John (1955)
10 Norman, Greg (1955)
11 Brandy (1979)
12 Blume, Judy (1938)
15 Groening, Matt (1954)
17 Anderson, Marian (1897)
Hargreaves, Alison (1962)
Jordan, Michael (1963)
18 Morrison, Toni (1931)
20 Adams, Ansel (1902)
Barkley, Charles (1963)

Cobain, Kurt (1967)
Crawford, Cindy (1966)
21 Carpenter, Mary Chapin (1958)
Jordan, Barbara (1936)
24 Jobs, Steven (1955)
Whitestone, Heather (1973)
25 Voigt, Cynthia (1942)
27 Clinton, Chelsea (1980)
28 Andretti, Mario (1940)
Pauling, Linus (1901)

March

1 Murie, Olaus J. (1889)
Rabin, Yitzhak (1922)
Zamora, Pedro (1972)
2 Gorbachev, Mikhail (1931)
Seuss, Dr. (1904)
3 Hooper, Geoff (1979)
Joyner-Kersee, Jackie (1962)
MacLachlan, Patricia (1938)
5 Margulis, Lynn (1938)
10 Guy, Jasmine (1964)
Miller, Shannon (1977)
12 Hamilton, Virginia (1936)
13 Van Meter, Vicki (1982)
15 Ginsburg, Ruth Bader (1933)
16 O'Neal, Shaquille (1972)
17 Nureyev, Rudolf (1938)
18 Blair, Bonnie (1964)
de Klerk, F.W. (1936)
Queen Latifah (1970)
20 Lee, Spike (1957)
22 Shatner, William (1931)
25 Lovell, Jim (1928)
Steinem, Gloria (1934)
26 O'Connor, Sandra Day (1930)
27 Carey, Mariah (1970)
28 James, Cheryl
McEntire, Reba (1955)
30 Hammer (1933)
31 Chavez, Cesar (1927)
Gore, Al (1948)

April

1 Maathai, Wangari (1940)
2 Carvey, Dana (1955)
3 Garth, Jennie (1972)
Goodall, Jane (1934)
4 Angelou, Maya (1928)

April, continued

5 Powell, Colin (1937)
6 Watson, James D. (1928)
7 Dougals, Marjory Stoneman (1890)
12 Cleary, Beverly (1916)
Doherty, Shannen (1971)
Letterman, David (1947)
13 Brandis, Jonathan (1976)
14 Rose, Pete (1941)
16 Abdul-Jabbar, Kareem (1947)
Selena (1971)
Williams, Garth (1912)
17 Champagne, Larry III (1985)
18 Hart, Melissa Joan (1976)
22 Levi-Montalcini, Rita (1909)
Oppenheimer, J. Robert (1904)
25 Fitzgerald, Ella (1917)
26 Pei, I.M. (1917)
28 Baker, James (1930)
Duncan, Lois (1934)
Hussein, Saddam (1937)
Leno, Jay (1950)
29 Agassi, Andre (1970)
Seinfeld, Jerry (1954)

May

2 Spock, Benjamin (1903)
7 Land, Edwin (1909)
9 Bergen, Candice (1946)
10 Jamison, Judith (1944)
11 Farrakhan, Louis (1933)
13 Rodman, Dennis (1961)
14 Smith, Emmitt (1969)
15 Johns, Jasper (1930)
Zindel, Paul (1936)
17 Paulsen, Gary (1939)
18 John Paul II (1920)
21 Robinson, Mary (1944)
23 Bardeen, John (1908)
O'Dell, Scott (1898)
26 Ride, Sally (1951)
27 Carson, Rachel (1907)
Kerr, M.E. (1927)

June

1 Lalas, Alexi (1970)
4 Kistler, Darci (1964)
5 Scarry, Richard (1919)
6 Rylant, Cynthia (1954)
7 Oleynik, Larisa (1981)

8 Bush, Barbara (1925)
Edelman, Marian Wright (1939)
Wayans, Keenen Ivory (1958)
Wright, Frank Lloyd (1869)
10 Sendak, Maurice (1928)
11 Cousteau, Jacques (1910)
Montana, Joe (1956)
12 Bush, George (1924)
13 Allen, Tim (1953)
Christo (1935)
14 Bourke-White, Margaret (1904)
Graf, Steffi (1969)
15 Horner, Jack (1946)
16 McClintock, Barbara (1902)
17 Gingrich, Newt (1943)
Jansen, Dan (1965)
18 Morris, Nathan (1971)
Van Allsburg, Chris (1949)
19 Abdul, Paula (1962)
Aung San Suu Kyi (1945)
20 Goodman, John (1952)
21 Bhutto, Benazir (1953)
Breathed, Berke (1957)
22 Bradley, Ed (1941)
23 Rudolph, Wilma (1940)
Thomas, Clarence (1948)
25 Carle, Eric (1929)
Gibbs, Lois (1951)
26 LeMond, Greg (1961)
27 Babbitt, Bruce (1938)
Perot, H. Ross (1930)

July

1 Brower, David (1912)
Diana, Princess of Wales (1961)
Duke, David (1950)
Lewis, Carl (1961)
McCully, Emily Arnold (1939)
2 Marshall, Thurgood (1908)
Thomas, Dave (1932)
5 Watterson, Bill (1958)
7 Chagall, Marc (1887)
9 Hanks, Tom (1956)
Krim, Mathilde (1926)
10 Ashe, Arthur (1943)
Boulmerka, Hassiba (1969)
11 Cisneros, Henry (1947)
White, E.B. (1899)
12 Cosby, Bill (1937)
Yamaguchi, Kristi (1972)

July, continued
13 Stewart, Patrick (1940)
15 Aristide, Jean-Bertrand (1953)
16 Sanders, Barry (1968)
18 Mandela, Nelson (1918)
20 Hillary, Sir Edmund (1919)
21 Reno, Janet (1938)
    Williams, Robin (1952)
22 Calder, Alexander (1898)
    Dole, Bob (1923)
    Hinton, S.E. (1948)
24 Krone, Julie (1963)
    Wilson, Mara (1987)
26 Berenstain, Jan (1923)
28 Davis, Jim (1945)
29 Burns, Ken (1953)
    Dole, Elizabeth Hanford (1936)
    Jennings, Peter (1938)
    Morris, Wanya (1973)
30 Hill, Anita (1956)
    Moore, Henry (1898)
    Schroeder, Pat (1940)
31 Reid Banks, Lynne (1929)

August
 1 Brown, Ron (1941)
    Coolio (1963)
    Garcia, Jerry (1942)
 2 Baldwin, James (1924)
    Healy, Bernadine (1944)
 3 Roper, Dee Dee
 5 Ewing, Patrick (1962)
 6 Robinson, David (1965)
    Warhol, Andy (1928?)
 7 Duchovny, David (1960)
    Leakey, Louis (1903)
 9 Anderson, Gillian (1968)
    Houston, Whitney (1963)
    Sanders, Deion (1967)
    Travers, P.L. (1899?)
11 Haley, Alex (1921)
    Hogan, Hulk (1953)
12 Martin, Ann M. (1955)
    Myers, Walter Dean (1937)
    Sampras, Pete (1971)
13 Battle, Kathleen (1948)
    Castro, Fidel (1927)
14 Berry, Halle (1967?)
    Johnson, Magic (1959)
    Larson, Gary (1950)

15 Ellerbee, Linda (1944)
18 Murie, Margaret (1902)
19 Clinton, Bill (1946)
    Soren, Tabitha (1967)
20 Chung, Connie (1946)
22 Schwarzkopf, H. Norman (1934)
23 Novello, Antonia (1944)
    Phoenix, River (1970)
24 Arafat, Yasir (1929)
    Ripken, Cal, Jr. (1960)
26 Burke, Christopher (1965)
    Culkin, Macaulay (1980)
    Sabin, Albert (1906)
28 Dove, Rita (1952)
    Evans, Janet (1971)
    Peterson, Roger Tory (1908)
    Priestley, Jason (1969)
30 Earle, Sylvia (1935)
31 Perlman, Itzhak (1945)

September
 1 Estefan, Gloria (1958)
 2 Bearden, Romare (1912?)
    Galeczka, Chris (1981)
 5 Guisewite, Cathy (1950)
 7 Lawrence, Jacob (1917)
    Moses, Grandma (1860)
    Pippig, Uta (1965)
 8 Prelutsky, Jack (1940)
    Thomas, Jonathan Taylor (1982)
13 Johnson, Michael (1967)
    Taylor, Mildred D. (1943)
15 Marino, Dan (1961)
16 Dahl, Roald (1916)
17 Burger, Warren (1907)
18 de Mille, Agnes (1905)
    Fields, Debbi (1956)
21 Fielder, Cecil (1963)
    King, Stephen (1947)
23 Nevelson, Louise (1899)
24 Ochoa, Severo (1905)
25 Locklear, Heather (1961)
    Lopez, Charlotte (1976)
    Pippen, Scottie (1965)
    Reeve, Christopher (1952)
    Smith, Will (1968)
    Walters, Barbara (1931)
26 Stockman, Shawn (1972)
27 Handford, Martin (1956)
29 Berenstain, Stan (1923)
    Guey, Wendy (1983)

203

October

1 Carter, Jimmy (1924)
2 Leibovitz, Annie (1949)
3 Herriot, James (1916)
   Winfield, Dave (1951)
5 Hill, Grant (1972)
   Lemieux, Mario (1965)
7 Ma, Yo-Yo (1955)
8 Jackson, Jesse (1941)
   Ringgold, Faith (1930)
   Stine, R.L. (1943)
9 Bryan, Zachery Ty (1981)
10 Saro-Wiwa, Ken (1941)
11 Perry, Luke (1964?)
   Young, Steve (1961)
12 Childress, Alice (1920?)
   Ward, Charlie (1970)
13 Kerrigan, Nancy (1969)
   Rice, Jerry (1962)
14 Daniel, Beth (1956)
15 Iacocca, Lee A. (1924)
17 Jemison, Mae (1956)
18 Foreman, Dave (1946)
   Marsalis, Wynton (1961)
   Navratilova, Martina (1956)
20 Mantle, Mickey (1931)
21 Gillespie, Dizzy (1956)
23 Pelé (1940)
26 Clinton, Hillary Rodham (1947)
27 Anderson, Terry (1947)
28 Gates, Bill (1955)
   Salk, Jonas (1914)
29 Ryder, Winona (1971)
31 Candy, John (1950)
   Pauley, Jane (1950)

November

2 lang, k.d. (1961)
3 Arnold, Roseanne (1952)
8 Mittermeier, Russell A. (1949)
9 Denton, Sandi
   Sagan, Carl (1934)
11 Vonnegut, Kurt (1922)
12 Andrews, Ned (1980)

   Harding, Tonya (1970)
13 Goldberg, Whoopi (1949)
14 Boutros-Ghali, Boutros (1922)
15 O'Keeffe, Georgia (1887)
16 Baiul, Oksana (1977)
17 Fuentes, Daisy (1966)
18 Mankiller, Wilma (1945)
19 Strug, Kerri (1977)
21 Aikman, Troy (1966)
   Griffey, Ken, Jr. (1969)
   Speare, Elizabeth George (1908)
24 Ndeti, Cosmas (1971)
25 Grant, Amy (1960)
   Thomas, Lewis (1913)
26 Pine, Elizabeth Michele (1975)
   Schulz, Charles (1922)
27 White, Jaleel (1977)
29 L'Engle, Madeleine (1918)
30 Jackson, Bo (1962)
   Parks, Gordon (1912)
 ? Pike, Christopher (1954)

December

2 Macaulay, David (1946)
   Seles, Monica (1973)
   Watson, Paul (1950)
3 Filipovic, Zlata (1980)
7 Bird, Larry (1956)
8 Rivera, Diego (1886)
12 Bialik, Mayim (1975)
   Frankenthaler, Helen (1928)
13 Fedorov, Sergei (1969)
15 Mendes, Chico (1944)
16 McCary, Michael (1971)
18 Sanchez Vicario, Arantxa (1971)
   Spielberg, Steven (1947)
21 Evert, Chris (1954)
   Griffith Joyner, Florence (1959)
22 Pinkney, Jerry (1939)
23 Avi (1937)
26 Butcher, Susan (1954)
27 Roberts, Cokie (1943)
28 Washington, Denzel (1954)
30 Woods, Tiger (1975)

People to Appear in Future Issues

Actors
Trini Alvarado
Richard Dean
  Anderson
Dan Aykroyd
Tyra Banks
Drew Barrymore
Levar Burton
Cher
Kevin Costner
Courtney Cox
Tom Cruise
Jamie Lee Curtis
Patti D'Arbanville-
  Quinn
Geena Davis
Ozzie Davis
Ruby Dee
Michael De Lorenzo
Matt Dillon
Michael Douglas
Larry Fishburne
Harrison Ford
Jody Foster
Morgan Freeman
Richard Gere
Tracey Gold
Graham Greene
Mark Harmon
Michael Keaton
Val Kilmer
Angela Lansbury
Joey Lawrence
Martin Lawrence
Christopher Lloyd
Kellie Martin
Marlee Matlin
Bette Midler
Alyssa Milano
Demi Moore
Rick Moranis
Tamera Mowry
Tia Mowry
Kate Mulgrew
Eddie Murphy
Liam Neeson
Leonard Nimoy
Rosie O'Donnell
Sean Penn
Phylicia Rashad
Keanu Reeves
Jason James Richter
Julia Roberts
Bob Saget
Arnold
  Schwarzenegger
Alicia Silverstone
Christian Slater
Taran Noah Smith

Jimmy Smits
Wesley Snipes
Sylvester Stallone
John Travolta
Mario Van Peebles
Damon Wayans
Bruce Willis
B.D. Wong
Malik Yoba

Artists
Mitsumasa Anno
Graeme Base
Maya Ying Lin
Yoko Ono

Astronauts
Neil Armstrong

Authors
Jean M. Auel
Gwendolyn Brooks
John Christopher
Arthur C. Clarke
John Colville
Paula Danziger
Paula Fox
Patricia Reilly Gibb
Jamie Gilson
Rosa Guy
Nat Hentoff
Norma Klein
E.L. Konigsburg
Lois Lowry
Stephen Manes
Norma Fox Mazer
Anne McCaffrey
Gloria D. Miklowitz
Marsha Norman
Robert O'Brien
Francine Pascal
Daniel Pinkwater
Ann Rice
Louis Sachar
John Saul
Shel Silverstein
Amy Tan
Alice Walker
Jane Yolen
Roger Zelazny

Business
Minoru Arakawa
Michael Eisner
David Geffen
Wayne Huizenga
Donna Karan
Phil Knight

Estee Lauder
Sheri Poe
Anita Roddick
Donald Trump
Ted Turner
Lillian Vernon

Cartoonists
Lynda Barry
Roz Chast
Greg Evans
Nicole Hollander
Art Spiegelman
Garry Trudeau

Comedians
Billy Crystal
Steve Martin
Eddie Murphy
Bill Murray

Dancers
Debbie Allen
Mikhail Baryshnikov
Gregory Hines
Twyla Tharp
Tommy Tune

Directors/Producers
Woody Allen
Steven Bocho
Tim Burton
Francis Ford Coppola
Ron Howard
John Hughes
George Lucas
Penny Marshall
Leonard Nimoy
Rob Reiner
John Singleton
Quentin Tarantino

Environmentalists/ Animal Rights
Kathryn Fuller
Linda Maraniss
Ingrid Newkirk
Pat Potter

Journalists
Tom Brokaw
John Hockenberry
Ted Koppel
Jim Lehrer
Dan Rather
Nina Totenberg
Mike Wallace
Bob Woodward

Musicians
Ace of Base
Babyface
Basia
George Benson
Bjork
Clint Black
Ruben Blades
Mary J. Blige
Bono
Edie Brickell
James Brown
Ray Charles
Chayanne
Natalie Cole
Cowboy Junkies
Sheryl Crow
Billy Ray Cyrus
Melissa Etheridge
Aretha Franklin
Green Day
Guns N' Roses
P.J. Harvey
Hootie & the Blowfish
India
Janet Jackson
Michael Jackson
Winona Judd
R. Kelly
Anthony Kiedis
Lenny Kravitz
Kris Kross
James Levine
LL Cool J
Andrew Lloyd
  Webber
Courtney Love
Lyle Lovett
MC Lyte
Madonna
Barbara Mandrell
Branford Marsalis
Paul McCartney
Midori
Alanis Morissette
Morrissey
N.W.A.
Jesseye Norman
Sinead O'Connor
Luciano Pavoratti
Pearl Jam
Teddy Pendergrass
David Pirner
Prince
Public Enemy
Raffi
Bonnie Raitt
Red Hot Chili
  Peppers

205

Lou Reed
L.A. Reid
R.E.M.
Trent Reznor
Kenny Rogers
Axl Rose
Run-D.M.C.
Paul Simon
Smashing Pumpkins
Sting
Michael Stipe
Pam Tillis
TLC
Randy Travis
Terence Trent d'Arby
Travis Tritt
U2
Eddie Vedder
Stevie Wonder
Trisha Yearwood
Dwight Yoakum
Neil Young

Politics/World Leaders
Madeleine Albright
Harry A. Blackmun
Jesse Brown
Pat Buchanan
Mangosuthu Buthelezi
Violeta Barrios de Chamorro
Shirley Chisolm
Jean Chretien
Warren Christopher
Edith Cresson
Mario Cuomo
Dalai Lama

Mike Espy
Alan Greenspan
Vaclav Havel
Jack Kemp
Bob Kerrey
Kim Il-Sung
Coretta Scott King
John Major
Imelda Marcos
Slobodan Milosevic
Mother Theresa
Ralph Nader
Manuel Noriega
Hazel O'Leary
Leon Panetta
Federico Pena
Simon Peres
Robert Reich
Ann Richards
Richard Riley
Phyllis Schlafly
Donna Shalala
Desmond Tutu
Lech Walesa
Eli Weisel
Vladimir Zhirinovsky

Royalty
Charles, Prince of Wales
Duchess of York (Sarah Ferguson)
Queen Noor

Scientists
Sallie Baliunas
Avis Cohen
Donna Cox
Stephen Jay Gould

Mimi Koehl
Deborah Letourneau
Philippa Marrack
Helen Quinn
Barbara Smuts
Flossie Wong-Staal
Aslihan Yener
Adrienne Zihlman

Sports
Jim Abbott
Muhammad Ali
Michael Andretti
Boris Becker
Barry Bonds
Bobby Bonilla
Jose Canseco
Jennifer Capriati
Michael Chang
Roger Clemens
Randall Cunningham
Eric Davis
Clyde Drexler
John Elway
George Foreman
Zina Garrison
Anfernee Hardaway
Rickey Henderson
Evander Holyfield
Brett Hull
Raghib Ismail
Jim Kelly
Petr Klima
Willy Mays
Paul Molitor
Jack Nicklaus
Joe Paterno
Kirby Puckett
Pat Riley

Mark Rippien
Daryl Strawberry
Danny Sullivan
Vinnie Testaverde
Isiah Thomas
Mike Tyson
Steve Yzerman

Television Personalities
Andre Brown (Dr. Dre)
Katie Couric
Phil Donahue
Kathie Lee Gifford
Ed Gordon
Bryant Gumbel
Arsenio Hall
Ricki Lake
Joan Lunden
Dennis Miller
Diane Sawyer
Alison Stewart
Jon Stewart
Vanna White
Montel Williams
Paul Zaloom

Other
James Brady
Johnnetta Cole
David Copperfield
Jaimie Escalante
Jack Kevorkian
Wendy Kopp
Sister Irene Kraus
Jeanne White

ON-APPROVAL ORDER FORM

Please send the following on 60-day approval:

BIOGRAPHY TODAY SUBJECT SERIES

Copies

Biography Today Artists Series – Vol. 1 .... $34
  ❑ Enter as a standing order, 10% discount

Biography Today Author Series
____ Vol. 1 ____ Vol. 2 ____ Vol. 3 .... each $34
  ❑ Enter as a standing order, 10% discount

Biography Today Scientists and Inventors Series
____ Vol. 1 ____ Vol. 2 .... each $34
  ❑ Enter as a standing order, 10% discount

Biography Today Sports General Series
____ Vol. 1 ____ Vol. 2 .... each $34

Biography Today Sports Baseball Series — Vol. 1 ...... $34
Biography Today Sports Basketball Series — Vol. 1 ..... $34
Biography Today Sports Football Series — Vol. 1 ...... $34
  ❑ Enter as a standing order, 10% discount

Biography Today World Leader Series:
____ _Environmental Leaders_ – Vol. 1 .... $34
____ _Modern African Leaders_ – Vol. 2 .... $34
  ❑ Enter as a standing order, 10% discount

❑ Payment enclosed, ship postpaid   ❑ Bill us, plus shipping

Institution _____
Attention _____
Address _____
City _____
State, Zip _____
Phone (___) _____

02/97

We want to cover the people **you** want to know about in _Biography Today_. Take a look at the list of people we plan to include in upcoming issues. Then use this card to list other people you want to see in _**Biography Today**_. If we include someone you suggest, your library wins a free issue, and you get one to keep with our thanks.

People I'd like to see in BIOGRAPHY TODAY:

_____
_____
_____
_____
_____

Name _____
Institution _____
Address _____
City _____
State, Zip _____